THE
YELLOW BOOK
OF
GAMES
AND
ENERGIZERS

of related interest

101 Things to Do on the Street
Games and Resources for Detached, Outreach and Street-Based Youth Work
2nd edition
Vanessa Rogers
ISBN 978 1 84905 187 3

Once Upon a Group
A Guide to Running and Participating in Successful Groups
2nd edition
Maggie Kindred and Michael Kindred
ISBN 978 1 84905 166 8

Working with Young Women
Activities for Exploring Personal, Social and Emotional Issues
2nd edition
Vanessa Rogers
ISBN 978 1 84905 095 1

Working with Young Men
Activities for Exploring Personal, Social and Emotional Issues
2nd edition
Vanessa Rogers
ISBN 978 1 84905 101 9

Social Skills Games for Children
Deborah M. Plummer
Illustrated by Jane Serrurier
Foreword by Professor Jannet Wright
ISBN 978 1 84310 617 3

Playful Group Activities *for*
Exploring Identity, Community,
Emotions *and* More!

THE
YELLOW BOOK
OF
GAMES
AND
ENERGIZERS

JAYARAJA and ERWIN TIELEMANS

Illustrated by Philip Paquet

Jessica Kingsley Publishers
London and Philadelphia

First published in 2011
by Jessica Kingsley Publishers
116 Pentonville Road
London N1 9JB, UK
and
400 Market Street, Suite 400
Philadelphia, PA 19106, USA

www.jkp.com

Library of Congress Cataloging in Publication Data
Tielemans, Jayaraja.
 The yellow book of games and energizers : playful group activities for exploring identity,
community, emotions and more! / Jayaraja and Erwin Tielemans ; illustrated Philip Paquet.
  p. cm.
 ISBN 978-1-84905-193-4 (alk. paper)
 1. Group relations training. 2. Social groups. 3. Small groups. 4. Communication
in small groups. I. Tielemans, Erwin. II. Paquet, Philip. III. Title.
 HM1086.T54 2011
 302.3'4--dc22
                          2010043001

British Library Cataloguing in Publication Data
A CIP catalogue record for this book is available from the British Library

ISBN 978 1 84905 192 7

Printed and bound in Great Britain by
MPG Books Group

CONTENTS

PREFACE

In my probationary year as a P.E. and drama teacher in London I was often struck by the quality of learning, co-operation and fun the kids had during the break times. I pondered how I could harness that energy and joy in more formal learning environments. Thus began an odyssey of experimenting, collecting and researching games. After nearly 20 years it is a delight to come across a fellow seasoned adventurer in the educational value of play.

Jayaraja

As a monitor in youth movement I discovered the joy and the forming aspects of games. In my class I used games to enrich the learning of my pupils. For the last 15 years I have integrated games and playful activities into workshops for profit and non-profit organizations. Games give added value and often a very rich learning environment. I value very much the strong learning effects of these games in all kinds of training and workshops on social learning, communication and leadership skills.

Erwin Tielemans

This book is a collection of the many games we have used in our workshops and training over the last 20 years. Some of the games we have invented, or at least imagine we have; others we have played since our own childhood and we hope they will be played by many generations to come.

We would like to thank the many colleagues who over the years have introduced us to new games or creative variations of old favourites, and also the many people we have played with.

Our aim has been to collect these games together and present them in an accessible way for teachers, trainers and others who would like to enrich their work with playful games and ideas. We are pleased to say that we have failed to collect them all together in one volume and are now working on Volume 2, which includes sections on environmental, co-operative, and rough games, and more.

In the meantime we hope that this volume serves to inspire and support you in using the innate curiosity, playfulness and sociability inherent in games.

Jayaraja
Erwin Tielemans
August 2010

INTRODUCTION

In writing this book we wanted to give as much information as succinctly as possible. This introduction gives you the essential structure of the book.

Five chapters

The games are arranged in 5 different chapters, to help you find the games you need. We have ordered the games according to what we consider the level of risk. The low-risk ones are at the start of the chapter, the high-risk ones at the end of the chapter. A full alphabetical index of games is at the end of the book.

Instruction language

An important skill is to be able to explain the games quickly and clearly, so to help you **we have suggested in bold print verbal instructions for you to read out**. As you become more familiar with the games you will find your own words. It also helps enormously to use clear, expressive body language and to demonstrate when you introduce the game.

Technical aspects

For each game we have included technical information, such as:

- number of participants
- minimum age
- suggested length of the activity
- materials required
- energy level
- risk level.

The energy level gives a sense of how much energy is needed to play the game and/or how much energy you get from it.

The risk level indicates the kind of group the game is suitable for – for example with new groups (low level) or experienced or confident groups (high level).

Downloadable resources

All pages marked with a ✓ are available in large format for download at www.jkp.com/catalogue/book/9781849051927/resources.

TIPS FOR WORKING WITH ENERGIZER GAMES

If you have ever participated in an energizer game you will probably remember the fun and inspiration you got from it. With skilled trainers the process can look very simple, but there are important factors to consider before, during and after each game, session or workshop.

Before
Location
Is the energizer game safe and suitable for the group?

Find a space where you can form a circle with the whole group. The circle is an excellent way of bringing order and aids ease of instruction and demonstration.

Ensure that there are no hazards or obstacles in the middle of the space.

In a classroom you can put the tables and chairs to the side or at the end of the room, though you may also use the chairs to form the circle.

For some games it is better to be outdoors or in a gym. If you are outdoors check to see that the ground is safe, with no glass or dangerous potholes.

It is also important to be aware of your position within the circle. If you have your back to the sun the group will have to squint to see you. With a large group outdoors you may need to be conscious of the wind direction and other factors that make it difficult for the participants to hear you.

Silence sign
As far as possible speak at a normal level. Avoid talking very loudly, as this tends to generate a noisy group and you will soon lose your voice.

A useful ritual we use is the silence sign. Explain that when you put your hand in the air you would like everyone to do the same, to signal that you would like silence. Once the group has understood this you can save time, energy and your voice.

Passing is okay

Make it clear before you start that it is okay if participants want to sit and observe a game instead of participating. We recommend that after giving the instruction you check if everyone wants to participate. It is important that people participate from choice rather than thinking they have to.

Risk level

When choosing a game consider the risk level and the needs of the group. Start with low-risk activities, and decide when to increase the risk level by observing the group and learning from the debriefing.

Outline goal beforehand

Give a reason for doing an activity and an indication of what you want to achieve with it in general terms. Avoid saying what the learning effects will be or what participants will feel – that is something you can explore in the debriefing.

Instructions

Use short, clear sentences to tell the participants what to do. Practise the instructions before the session, formulating them in your own words or using the instructions suggested in this book (**in bold type**) as a guide.

Watch the participants' expressions while giving the instructions to gauge if they have understood, and then check if they have questions about the activity.

Where possible demonstrate and use your body language to support the verbal instructions. Practise and reflect on the outcome.

Long instructions

If a game is complex you can break it down into discrete stages, adding a new aspect each time. It is best to give no more than 3 things to do at a time, for example when you want participants to move around, ask them first to stand, then let them form groups, waiting until they have formed groups to give the next assignment…

Kindly language

Use invitational language when you give the instruction. Start with: 'I would like you to…', 'Please come and…' or 'May I invite you to…'

During

Participate

Participate as much as possible in the games. Your enthusiasm will affect the participants.

Of course, when you give the groups a problem to solve, you stay in the role of the observer.

If you need pairs for a game and the group is uneven, then join in, but if the group is even, stay at the side.

Stop if needed

If a game doesn't go as you anticipated, or if they have misunderstood your instructions, stop and give the instruction again.

Observe

Keep your eyes, ears and other senses active during a game. In this way you can relate your debriefing with what happened during the activity.

Stop before fun goes down

How long should a funny game last?

Stop it 10 seconds before it loses a bit of its magic. This means that there is always more fun to be had, and you finish each game having fun.

After

Reflection makes the difference! A simple game transforms into a valuable activity when the person who leads the game is able to help the group reflect on the activity. Most energizers have suggestions for the debriefing to enhance the learning and social development.

Open or closed

Mix open and closed questions in the debriefing. A closed question, requiring a yes-or-no answer, is easier than an open question.

For some participants it is wise to start with a closed question followed by an open one, a format you will often find in the book – for example, 'Did you see any relationship with this exercise and…? If so, what?'

If you use open questions you can relate them to the goal you mentioned before the game. You can focus your questions on different aspects:

- what participants feel
- what they think
- parallels and differences between the game and their experience in life
- what they have learnt or are learning
- how they will apply what is learnt in their own life.

As you become more experienced in using games to explore educational values, you can begin to adapt and/or use the games to address your specific aims with the group – for example, 'Mango mango' is a group-forming game and a fun game, but can also be used as a game to explore issues such as belonging, family, intergenerational relationships…

Ask everyone

If you ask questions, invite everyone to respond. Look at all participants and illustrate with your body language that the question is addressed to everyone.

Invite more than one participant to answer.

Avoid giving judgements on the answers. If an answer is not clear or is very abstract you might ask, 'I am not quite clear. Can you tell me what you mean?' or 'Can you give me an example?'

Treat each offering respectfully – it has meaning and purpose even though that may not be immediately obvious.

One question

Ask one question at a time, avoiding multiple questions like: 'How was this game? And what can you learn from it?'

Golden silence

When participants aren't used to answering open questions they will often have to think. Remain silent, trust that they are thinking and wait for the first person who wants to answer. If you talk you are likely to interrupt the creative process of thinking and reflection.

Keep it safe

In some groups participants can be reluctant to respond before the whole group. If you have long silences after your open questions, then form groups of 4 and ask the people to discuss the question in their group. The groups can write or draw their answers, which you can use for a plenary reflection.

Another safe way to reflect on your questions is discussion in pairs. If you ask your question and let them reflect in 2s or 3s, then participants will be more spontaneous.

Learn by doing

At the end of each session reflect, asking yourself questions to improve your ability in using games as a means for learning. The following questions might help:

- What went well?
- Did the game go as I wanted?
- What would I do the same?
- What would I do differently? How?
- Did the participants learn? What was helpful?
- Could I get more out of it? How?

ICEBREAKERS, TRUST AND COMMUNITY-BUILDING GAMES

Before a group of people can work well together, it helps if they get to know each other. The process of community building works best starting with low-risk activities. As trust builds, group members are more open to engage in activities where they share more personal information. As a facilitator it is important to respect the natural flow of group formation, moving sensitively from low-risk to high-risk activities. In this chapter you will find a collection of community-building activities of increasing order of risk.

I LIKE...
Good starter for large groups

Risk level: low

Energy level: medium

Number of participants: 12+

Age: 6+

Time: 5 minutes

Materials: none

Explanation

Participants sit in a circle.

> **'I want to invite you to exchange some information about yourselves. I will say something that I like and then stand up. If you also like the same thing, then you also stand up. If you are neutral or don't like the same thing, remain sitting.**
>
> **I like milk chocolate.'**

Look around to see who else stands up. Sit down and repeat this with other ideas, for example 'I like camping', 'I like cats', 'I like football', 'I like mountain walking'. Each time stand up and notice who else stands up.

Now invite members of the group to make statements in the same way: 'I like…', and then stand up and see who also likes what they like.

Comment

Keep to the structure of 'I like…', which encourages positive statements.

Debriefing

- How did you find this activity?
- Did you learn anything playing this game? And if so, what?
- How does this activity affect the atmosphere in the group?

VARIATION 1

A lower-risk version than standing is for participants to raise their hand if they like the same thing.

VARIATION 2

Do the activity standing. The trainer says: 'I like sports' and everyone who likes sports mimes the sport they like. For example:

- 'I like dancing.'
- 'I like gardening.'
- 'I like animals.'
- 'I like playing an instrument.'
- 'On holiday I like…'

MAP

Exchange personal information on an imaginary map

Risk level: low   *Age*: 10+
Energy level: medium   *Time*: 10 minutes
Number of participants: 10–50   *Materials*: none

Explanation

Participants stand in a circle.

Explain that the room is a big invisible map, pointing out north, south, east and west, and identifying some specific locations so that participants can easily visualize it.

> **'Find the place on the map where you currently live and then check those around you to see if you're in the right place.'**

When everyone has found their place, ask everyone where they come from.

> **'Now go to a spot on the map that you would like to visit.'**

Ask the participants where they would like to go and why.

Comment

This energizer is excellent for groups that come from a wide area. If participants come from different countries they may even ask each other to visit, or offer advice on what to see or do and what to avoid.

ROUND-UP
Forming circles according to specific criteria

45 36

Risk level: low

Energy level: medium

Number of participants: 15–50

Age: 6+

Time: 10 minutes

Materials: none

Explanation

Start in a circle.

> **'I'd like you to form a circle going clockwise from here according to how light or dark your shoes are...'**

Indicate the start and end point, according to the criteria for the round-up:

- from light to dark shoes
- from light to dark hair
- from blue to dark eyes
- alphabetical order of first name
- alphabetical order of last name
- according to the size of your hand
- according to shoe size

- from warm to cold hands (for this participants have to shake hands to find out)
- according to birthday
- according to house number
- according to how many years' experience you have in...
- alphabetical order of the first letter of your favourite food/hobby/ musician.

Comment

This energizer facilitates people making easy contact with each other, but avoid high-risk criteria such as weight, age, height...

Debriefing

- How did you find this activity?
- What effects did you experience?
- Did you find any activities easy?
- Was there anything you found difficult?
- Is there anything else that you would like to know about the others?

VARIATION

You can play the game with everyone standing on chairs or a bench, and they are not allowed to touch the ground as they endeavour to line up according to the given criteria. You can further increase the complexity by not allowing any talking.

If you don't have a bench or don't want to use chairs then make a 'small bridge' with masking tape. Ask the participants to imagine that the bridge hangs over a deep ravine.

ONE OF FOUR

Show what you like by moving in a square

Risk level: low
Energy level: medium
Number of participants: 12–40

Age: 8+
Time: 10 minutes
Materials: masking tape

Explanation

Make a square and divide it into a grid of 4 equal squares on the floor with masking tape. The participants stand around the square.

'In this game you have to choose from 4 words or concepts by standing in the appropriate box. I will say the 4 words and indicate which box is for which word. Make your choice, and when I clap my hands you stand in the appropriate box.'

Each time say 4 words and indicate a square for each word. Allow a moment and then clap your hands to stimulate quick choices.

Suggestions for words

red	green	yellow	blue
warm	dry	wet	cold
chicken	fish	beans	salad
bike	car	bus	walking
north	east	south	west
blond	brown	black	red
sports	maths	language	paint
happy	sad	angry	scared
bear	water	lemonade	milk
spring	summer	autumn	winter
dog	cat	rabbit	mouse
Jesus	Mohamed	Brahma	Buddha
village	city	beach	mountain
speak	write	listen	read

Comment

As the game proceeds it is good to ask in a general way: 'Is there anyone who would like to say why they made their particular choice?'

Debriefing

- Which choices were easy to make?
- What was difficult?
- Did anything surprise you, and if so, what?
- Were you affected by others in your choices, and if so, how?

REMEMBER MY NAME
An aid for memorizing everyone's name

Joe
(sounds like toe)

Florence
(Nightingale)

Charlie
(from Chaplin)

Nelson

Risk level: low
Energy level: low
Number of participants: 10–50

Age: 8+
Time: 10 minutes
Materials: none

Explanation

Participants sit in a circle.

> **'Think of an aid to help others remember your name. For example, my name is Jayaraja. It starts with a J and an A and ends the same way. In the middle it is "ya" and "ra" and my name means "victorious" (Jaya) "king" (raja): "Jayaraja."'**

Give the participants time to think of an aid to memorize their name.

When everyone is ready ask someone to start. The rest listen and try to remember each name.

When everyone has presented their name go around the circle and say each name in turn. If you can't remember, ask for the aid again.

Comment

It is good to follow this game with another game where participants have to use each others' names.

Debriefing

- How was it to find an aid to memorize your name?
- Which names do you find easiest to remember and why?
- What else do you think could help?

VARIATION

Participants stand in a circle. Everyone says their name before the group and makes a movement to underline a personal skill or quality. The group repeats the name and the movement.

DEBRIEFING

- How was it to say your name in this way in the group?
- How did it feel when you hear the group saying your name?

CONGREGATE
Community building by moving according to personal attributes and qualities

Risk level: low
Energy level: medium
Number of participants: 15–50

Age: 6+
Time: 10 minutes
Materials: none

Explanation

Participants stand in a circle.

> **'Form groups with people who are wearing the same colour as you.'**

When the groups are formed ask each group what is the colour that unites them.

> **'Now form a circle alphabetically according to your first name, starting with "A" at 12 o'clock.'**

When the circle is formed ask everyone to say their name, beginning with 'A'. Suggest the following criteria for forming groups:

- make groups with people who have the same hobbies
- line up according to your birthday with 1 January at point 'A' and 31 December at point 'B'. Indicate points A and B or suggest clear directions based on the set-up of the room

- form a group with people who like the same dessert as yourself
- line up according to the colour of your hair (from dark to light)
- form a group with people who give the same answer to the following statement: 'An important quality in a friend is...'

Comment

Progressively build up the level of risk.

Debriefing

- How was it to get to know each other in this way?
- What, if anything, did you find easy to do?
- What was more difficult?
- What else would you like to know about the other group members?

PROGRESSIVE DINNER
Short conversation in different groups

Risk level: low

Energy level: medium

Number of participants: 10–50

Age: 10+

Time: 10 minutes

Materials: none

Explanation

Participants stand in a circle.

> **'As a community-building activity I would like to invite you to a 4-course meal. With each course we will sit with a completely new group and discuss a new topic. First, let's walk around the room using all the space.**
>
> **For the starter, form groups of 5.'**

Participants form groups of 5.

> **'During the starter, talk about your favourite free-time activity. You have 1 minute in total and make sure everyone gets the chance to speak.'**

After a minute interrupt the activity, invite participants to thank their tablemates and once again walk around the room.

Next, form groups of 4 for the soup. During the soup the group exchanges ideas about a favourite holiday. Available time: 2 minutes.

Repeat this activity for:

- *the main dish*: 6 participants. What do I enjoy in my work/at school? Available time: 3 minutes.

- *dessert*: 4 participants. What were my expectations for this class/workshop? Available time: 3 minutes.

Debriefing

- How did you find this 'dinner'?
- What other ideas would you like to explore?
- What expectations were expressed in the last round?

BEHIND THE CURTAIN
Say the opponent's name first

Risk level: low
Energy level: high
Number of participants: 10–40

Age: 4+
Time: 10 minutes
Materials: bed sheet, 2 hats

Explanation

Divide into 2 equal groups, each group with one hat. Hold the sheet up between the 2 groups so neither group can see the other. You need either to secure one end of the sheet or to have an assistant to hold the sheet up.

> **'Each group chooses one person to put the hat on. When both teams are ready, we'll let the curtain drop. The aim is to call out the name of the opposite team member who is wearing the hat, and the first person to do this wins a point for their team.'**

Play the game several times. Encourage the players to be creative to make it more difficult for the opposition to get the name first, for example covering their face, standing with their back to the curtain, looking between their legs at the opponent...

Debriefing

- How did you find this game?

- How was it when you stood in the middle?

VARIATION 1

Two teams on either side of the room. Have all team members close their eyes whilst you choose one person from each team. Place these players in the middle, back-to-back so that they cannot see each other. The other team members open their eyes and give hints to their player about who their opponent is. The first one to say the other player's name wins a point for their team.

VARIATION 2

Same as Variation 1 but the teams can only use body language and mime to help their team mate.

WHO'S AWAY? (SMILE FOR THE CAMERA)

One member of the group pretends to be a photographer who has to spot who goes missing

Risk level: low

Energy level: medium

Number of participants: 12–40

Age: 8+

Time: 10 minutes

Explanation

Participants imagine they are going to have a group photo and one person volunteers to be the photographer.

To the photographer:

'Look at the group. Make a mental picture of them and then close your eyes. When your eyes are closed someone in the group will disappear.'

When the photographer closes his eyes point to someone in the group, who must quickly hide away. When the person is hidden you ask the photographer to open their eyes and see if they can see who is missing.

When groups do not yet know each others' names it is only necessary to indicate where the person has gone from. For groups that know each other the photographer must name the missing person.

Comment

Keep the time brief (maximum 10 seconds). The photographer does not need to leave the room, just close their eyes.

VARIATION 1

Vary this game. For example:

- remove 2 or 3 people
- have people change places in pairs
- have more than one photographer – the photographers can compete with each other
- with a small group, people can swap an item or 2 of clothing
- have everyone change places (as a joke).

VARIATION 2

With 6–12 people split the group into 2 equal teams, with each person sitting opposite an opponent.

The groups sit and look at each other for a minute or 2 and then turn away. Then each member of the team changes 3 visible things about themselves, drawing on the resources of other members of their team, for example someone may swap a tie or a belt with another member, or their glasses. When both teams are ready they sit again facing each other and try to spot the differences in their opponent.

PICTURE STORY
Using images to communicate aspects of ourselves

Risk level: low

Energy level: low

Number of participants: 12–40

Age: 8+

Time: 10 minutes

Materials: a large selection of images, pictures, postcards

Explanation

Spread the pictures on the ground in a circle and invite the participants to walk around them.

What you wish to explore with the group will determine what you say to them.

For community building:

'**Find an image that:**

- **says something about yourself**

- **says something about how you feel at the moment.**

Also find 2 images that relate to some aspects of your character.'

For dealing with conflict management:

> **'Find an image that represents something about conflict.**
>
> **Find an image that gives you ideas on how to deal with conflicts.**
>
> **Find an image that tells you something about escalation in conflicts.'**

When participants have chosen their images, each person in turn talks about the significance of the images for them. The rest of the group can ask questions.

Comment

You can ask the participants either to select the images from the collection or just to choose them mentally without taking them. Then others can choose the same image.

VARIATION

Spread 30 images around the room and ask everyone to walk around without speaking. When everyone has seen the pictures, you might say:

- 'Stand by a picture you like.'
- 'Stand by a picture that gives you pleasant feelings.'
- 'Stand by a picture that reminds you of something unpleasant.'

Each time you can give the participants a minute to talk about why they have chosen a picture. Those who are by a picture on their own can share with others who are also alone.

INFLATABLE HELICOPTER
Exploring expectations in a creative way

Risk level: low–medium
Energy level: low
Number of participants: 6–30

Age: 6+
Time: 5–10 minutes
Materials: a sack, bag or box

Explanation

Participants sit in a circle with a magic bag in the middle. (Try to have an attractive sack or bag, although you can always mime a bag.)

> **'On the first round I invite you to walk into the middle and say "I meant to bring a…", and then make an excuse for why you didn't. For example: "I meant to bring an inflatable helicopter but they didn't have one in the right colour."'**

After your example, participants enter the circle at random. This enables them to engage in their own time or to observe, which enhances the sense of safety. When everyone who wanted to say something has done so, give the following instruction:

> **'On the second round you can walk into the circle and say what you did bring, which can be 2 or 3 things or qualities. For example, "I am pleased to say that I did bring some enthusiasm, humour and a pen."'**

Again, when everyone who wants to has spoken, announce the third round:

'On the third round you say what you are hoping to get from the session or the day, for example: "I am hoping to get some inspiration, learning and fun."'

When all participants have finished, say thanks as a signal that the activity is over.

VARIATION 1

This game can be used as a name game in which people have forgotten to bring something that helps others remember their name. For example, 'I am Dave and I meant to bring a **d**iamond but I **d**ropped it down the **d**rain.'

VARIATION 2

The participants do all 3 rounds in one go, stepping into the middle and saying, 'I meant to bring…', 'I did bring…' and 'I hope to get…'

NAME BALL
A name game with a ball

Risk level: low–medium
Energy level: high
Number of participants: 10–30

Age: 8+
Time: 10 minutes
Materials: 3 soft balls, name tags

Explanation

Start in a circle with each participant wearing a name tag.

First round: Give the ball to someone.

'Say someone's name, throw the ball to them and then sit down. You can only throw to people who are standing.'

When everyone is sitting down move to the second round.

Second round: Give 3 people a ball each.

'This is the same game except this time we have 3 balls, so say a person's name, throw the ball to them and sit down.'

When everyone is sitting, move to the third round.

Third round: Everyone turns their name tag on upside down. Now give 3 people a ball each.

'This is the same game, so say a person's name, throw the ball to them and sit down.'

When everyone is sitting, move to the fourth round.

Fourth round: Everyone hides their name tag. Give 3 participants a ball each.

> **'Once again the same game, so say the person's name, throw the ball to them and sit down. If you can't remember someone's name you can ask for help.'**

When everyone is sitting, move to the fifth round.

Fifth round: No name tags. Give one participant a ball.

> **'In this round you can throw the ball to anyone standing or sitting. Again, say their name before throwing them the ball, and then sit down. When you catch the ball, say thank you and the name of the thrower. If you are seated and you can't say the name of the thrower, you must once again stand up. The goal is to remain seated.'**

Gradually introduce more balls into the circle.

When everyone is sitting, the game is over.

Comment

This is a good game to practise names in a light way.

The rules of the fifth round are a little more complex so perhaps run through the rules in 'slow motion'.

VARIATION

If participants already know each others' names, then people can invent a new name for themselves.

SECRET FRIEND
Do kind and generous things secretly for someone

Risk level: low–medium
Energy level: low
Number of participants: 12–100
Age: 6+

Time: a few days
Materials: a sheet of paper per person

Explanation

Give every participant a sheet of paper and a pencil.

> **'We are going to be together for…days and we are going to play a game where we become a secret friend to someone else. The aim is to be as kind and generous a friend as possible without them knowing who it is that is being so thoughtful to them.**
>
> **Because we all have different tastes we will give our secret friends some clues about what we like. Write down your name and at least 3 things that make you happy, that you enjoy or make life feel good.'**

Collect the papers, fold them and put them in a bowl, then allow people to pick one at random. If they get their own, they put it back and choose another one.

> **'Here are some ideas about how you can give a treat to your secret friend without them discovering your identity:**

- **You can ask others to give them a present or a letter.**

- **You can leave something on their chair or bed.**

- **You can observe them and see what other things they like, or ask their friends.**

- **You can write them a letter saying what you appreciate about them.'**

Usually participants find creative ways to fulfil their tasks. In groups with younger participants you may have to ask what they have done or what ideas they have, or make suggestions to inspire them.

To support communication with the secret friends you can organize an internal postal system. This way the participants can send letters to each other and also to their secret friend. Collect the letters in a 'friendly post-box' and distribute the letters at dinner.

Comment

This is an excellent exercise to promote awareness of others and also to create a friendly atmosphere in a group. It is also fun and playful. The debriefing is an important part of the celebration, learning and enjoyment of the exercise. The exercise can be used in a classroom over the period of the year, with people picking a new secret friend each term or half term. The debriefing can be an excellent way to draw the term to a close.

Debriefing

At the end of the event or time span, formally bring the secret friend game to a close. Get everyone sitting in a circle and ask people to celebrate what kind and friendly acts they appreciated over their time together, and then ask them to guess who they think their secret friend was. Allow some time for the group to mingle, celebrate and thank each other.

- How did you find the game?

- What things did you enjoy doing for others?

- How did the game affect your way of being together?

THREE LETTERS
Share something about yourself using 3 letters

Risk level: low–medium
Energy level: low
Number of participants: 10–30
Age: 10+

Time: 10 minutes
Materials: cards that can
eventually be used as name tags,
markers

Explanation

Participants sit in a circle.

Give each participant a card and a marker.

> **'Write your name on one side. On the reverse write the first letter of 3 particular talents or characteristics you have, for example an M if you play music, an A if you are adventurous...'**

When everyone is ready, give the following instruction:

> **'Find a partner. Tell them your name and the 3 talents or characteristics relating to the letters on the reverse, then exchange cards, remembering what their letters stand for. Now find a new partner and repeat the process, passing on the information as accurately as possible and exchanging cards again. Do this a third time and then take a seat.'**

When all the participants are seated, invite them to present each other one by one, using the cards they have, checking that the information given is correct after each presentation. Now the participants can use the cards as name tags.

Comment

This is a quick icebreaker for groups that already know each other.

Debriefing

- How was it to choose 3 talents/characteristics?
- How was it to exchange cards?
- Having done this activity what strikes you about this group?

SPEAKER'S BALL
Use a ball to say something about yourself

Risk level: medium
Energy level: low
Number of participants: 12–40

Age: 6+
Time: 1 minute per participant
Materials: soft ball, name tags

Explanation

Participants sit in a circle with everyone wearing a clearly readable name tag. Copy the words in the picture above on to a flipchart as an aid for the group.

> **'When you get the ball you have the opportunity to present yourself to the group. Using the examples on the flipchart (though not exclusively), you have 1 minute to say something about yourself. After 1 minute say someone's name and pass the ball to them.'**

Start by presenting yourself to the group. Be conscious of the time, as the group will follow your example, so aim to be as clear and full as 1 minute will allow.

Comment

This is a high-risk activity, especially in large groups, as many people find it a challenge presenting themselves to a large group. Therefore it is best to use this game as the third or fourth activity for community building.

Debriefing

- How did you find listening to the others?
- Is there anything particular that stays in your mind?
- How was it to present yourself to the group?
- How does this exercise contribute to how you feel good in the group?

VARIATION

An easier version is to ask participants to say one thing about themselves, for example where they live, favourite music, favourite vacation, a particular interest…

COMMON CIRCLE
Finding similarities

Risk level: medium
Energy level: low
Number of participants: 12–40
Age: 8+

Time: 10 minutes
Materials: copies of template for each participant (for Variation 2)

Explanation

Participants sit in a circle, numbering off around the circle, 1, 2, 1, 2, 1, 2…and so on.

> **'All the number 1s find one thing they have in common with the person on their left, perhaps an interest, a place you have both been, a sport you like or a book or film. Be creative in searching for something.'**

After 2 minutes the number 2s then repeat the process with the person on their left.

When everyone is ready, each person presents the common thing with their neighbour on the left. Continue round the circle until everyone has presented.

Comment

It is good to allow the participants 2 minutes to find something in common.

VARIATION 1

Everyone looks for 2 interesting differences and 2 things they have in common. Allow about 10 minutes and then each person in turn presents the differences and the things they have in common. This variation is good with smaller groups.

VARIATION 2

Download the template (see next page) from www.jkp.com/catalogue/book/9781849051927/resources, make a copy for each participant and hand them out.

> **'Form pairs and find 3 things you have in common and 3 differences with your partner. When you are ready, find someone else and do the same, repeating this with 3 different people.'**

When you are finished, sit down in the circle. When everyone is ready, each person mentions the most interesting similarity and difference.

COMMENT

An excellent exercise to begin a workshop/lesson about cultural differences.

Common circle

Form pairs with 3 members of the group, and find 3 things you have in common and 3 differences.

With . . . .

I have these things in common:

1. . . . .
2. . . . .
3. . . . .

And these differences:

1. . . . .
2. . . . .
3. . . . .

With . . . .

I have these things in common:

1. . . . .
2. . . . .
3. . . . .

And these differences:

1. . . . .
2. . . . .
3. . . . .

With . . . .

I have these things in common:

1. . . . .
2. . . . .
3. . . . .

And these differences:

1. . . . .
2. . . . .
3. . . . .

TALK NOW

Participants have short conversations on specific subjects

Risk level: medium

Energy level: medium

Number of participants: 10–100

Age: 10+

Time: 20 minutes

Materials: none

Explanation

Participants stand in a circle.

> 'In this exercise we going to have short conversations in pairs with people we would like to get to know better. Look around the circle and think who you want to talk to. Make a choice – 3, 2, 1, go!'

When they are in pairs, give the following instruction.

> 'You may not have met the person you wanted, but don't worry, we will play this game at least 3 more times. For now here are some strict rules for this communication game.
>
> I would like you to talk for 1 minute about a specific subject which I will suggest.
>
> The listening partner endeavours to listen as fully as possible, though asking questions is allowed.

> **Each time I will give a criterion which determines who speaks first.**
>
> **When the minute is over I will give a sign, and you switch roles.**
>
> **After the conversation you thank your partner, shake hands, and say goodbye, and on my signal find a new partner for the next conversation.'**

Each time give a subject to talk about and the criterion to determine who speaks first.

Subject suggestions	Who starts talking?
Favourite holiday.	The person with the highest house number.
What I like doing in my free time.	Who got up earliest that morning?
What makes me happy?	The person who lives furthest away.
What do I expect from this course/ school year?	The person with the longest index finger.

Comment

- You can choose subjects related to the lesson or workshop you are giving and use this activity as an introduction to a specific subject.

- Reduce the speaking time (30 seconds) for groups that aren't used to talking.

- In the debriefing, participants often comment that the time and subject restrictions inhibit the flow of conversation. This can be the starting point for a discussion on the ingredients of good conversation.

Debriefing

- How did you find this activity?

- How was it to listen for a minute?

- How was it to talk for a minute?

- Who would you like to talk to and about what?

VARIATION 1

If you want to introduce a random element to the paired conversation it is easily done by having a double circle (see picture). After the completion of each conversation the outer circle moves one space clockwise and the inner circle one space anti-clockwise.

The random pairing can facilitate a greater sense of ease and is particularly helpful when working with a mixed group of boys and girls, or when there is the potential for certain group members not to be selected.

VARIATION 2

For 12+ participants. Ask participants to use their keys as the starting point for the conversation. Invite the speakers to talk about 'what precious/valuable things are safe, thanks to one of my keys'.

VARIATION 3

For 12+ participants. Each participant draws 3 symbols that are meaningful for them. They attach the symbols to themselves (with a pin or some tape) and these are the starting point for a conversation in pairs.

'You have 7 minutes to get to know each other a bit better. Begin with one symbol you each have drawn.'

After 7 minutes give a signal, and the participants move on to a new partner and follow the same structure.

GROUP POSTER
Pictures to present group members

Risk level: medium
Energy level: low
Number of participants: 12–40
Age: 6+

Time: 20 minutes
Materials: big sheets of paper,
colour markers

Explanation

Form groups of 6. Each group gets a big sheet and colour markers.

> **'Make a poster of the group, with each person drawing a picture of someone else in the group. First, interview a partner and choose 3 skills, qualities or characteristics to draw. Check if they're happy with the things you've suggested and then create your picture.'**

Allow 15 minutes for the interviews and drawings.

Hang the posters on the wall. Each person takes a turn at introducing a member of the group, using the poster as an aid. The members of the other groups try to guess who it is.

Comment

This activity is suitable for a group where the participants know each other quite well.

You can tailor the exercise to specific aspects that you may wish to explore in the group, for example:

- Present your partner using images that describe what they like to do on holiday or in their free time.

- Present your partner using images to represent their dreams and ambitions, within the group, team or organization.

Debriefing

- How was it to present the skills/characteristics of someone in a drawing?

- How was it to interview someone?

- Did you learn something from this activity, and if so, what?

SHAKE ELBOWS
Physical greeting

Risk level: medium
Energy level: medium
Number of participants: 10–40

Age: 6+
Time: 5 minutes
Materials: none

Explanation

Participants stand in a circle. Number off 1 to 4 around the circle.

> **'People with number 1 put their hands on their head. Number 2s put their hands on their shoulders. Number 3s put their hands on their waist, and number 4s put their hands on their knees.**
>
> **Now, keeping your hands where they are, I want you to greet each other by touching both elbows, saying each other's name, and wishing them a great day.'**

Give a quick demonstration to clarify the game.

The game finishes when everyone has greeted everyone else.

Comment

Low-risk game to start a session with participants that already know each other.

ATOM GAME

High-speed community building. Short contacts about everyday topics

Risk level: medium
Energy level: medium
Number of participants: 10–50

Age: 10+
Time: 10 minutes
Materials: none

Explanation

Participants stand in a circle.

> **'Imagine that you are an atom, moving around the room trying to find as much space as possible. When I call a number I want you to form molecules, which are groups of atoms of that number. Anyone left over, join the nearest molecule.'**

Encourage the participants to use the whole space and then call a number, for example, '6!' Participants form groups (molecules) of 6 as quickly as possible and any left over join the nearest group.

> **'In each group, starting with the tallest person and then going clockwise, say what your favourite food is. As soon as everyone in the molecule has spoken you all put your right hand in the middle.'**

When all the molecules/groups are ready, give the following instruction:

'The molecules are going to break down into atoms again. You will feel the energy shaking through the stack of hands and building to a crescendo of sound and energy, and on "boom" the atoms are once again blown apart and move around the room… 3, 2, 1 – "boom!"'

When everyone is once again moving around the room, call another number for the size of the molecules/groups, and when they are formed, give a subject, tell them who starts and the time available.

Molecule size	Subject	Who starts	Available time
6	Favourite food.	The tallest person.	30 seconds
7	Favourite book or film.	The shortest person.	1 minute
8	What you do in your free time.	The person with the lightest hair.	90 seconds
5	What kind of music you like.	The person with the darkest hair.	90 seconds
4	I am dreaming of…	The person who has the lowest house number.	90 seconds
3	My expectations for this workshop.	The person who has the highest house number.	2 minutes

Comment

This is a playful energizer suitable when you don't have much time for community building. With younger groups you can use water bubbles instead of atoms.

Debriefing

- How did you find this activity?
- How was it to say something about yourself in such a short space of time?
- How was it hearing from the other members of the group?
- Does this contribute to community building? And if so, how?
- Finally, what expectations were expressed in the last round?

ID CARD
Short conversations about self-made ID cards

Risk level: medium
Energy level: low
Number of participants: 12–50
Age: 10+
Time: 20 minutes

Materials: blank card for each person (see template for Variation 2), a flipchart/board with suggested ideas to include and a variety of pens

Explanation

Distribute blank business cards and pens.

'Create a personal ID card. There are some ideas on the board to help you but be creative –'

- a picture of yourself
- place where you live
- hobbies
- a skill you have
- favourite book
- favourite film
- what you do at the weekend
- sports.

Allow about 5 minutes to create the cards and then form random groups.

'Form groups of 5; you have a minute each to present yourself. I'll signal when 5 minutes are up.'

If there is enough time, invite everyone to present someone else using that person's ID card. The rest of the group try to guess who it is.

Comment

This is a high-risk exercise, best only introduced if the preceding exercises have gone well.

Debriefing

* How did you find this activity?

* How was it to tell/show something about yourself?

* How was it to hear from other participants?

* Did you learn anything playing this game and if so, what?

VARIATION 1

When everyone has their ID card ready they walk criss-cross around the room, and on a signal form pairs. Each person takes 1 minute to present themselves to their partner. Then repeat with 2 or 3 new partners.

VARIATION 2

Download the ID card at www.jkp.com/catalogue/book/9781849051 927/resources, print it out and give everyone a copy. Each person then fills that in and proceeds with the exercise of meeting and sharing with other group members the information about themselves.

VARIATION 3

Each participant draws a picture or makes a sculpture (with whatever material you think would be fun or relevant for the group) of themselves. When everyone is ready, participants present themselves in pairs or in small groups.

Ideas for pictures (or sculptures):

- My strong skills.
- What I like about other people.
- If you want something from me you'd better...
- What is very important to me.
- I find it hard to...

VARIATION 4

Make a drawing of your hand. On each finger write something about yourself, for example:

- *Thumb*: favourite food.
- *Index finger*: sport/hobby.
- *Middle finger*: an animal I like.
- *Ring finger*: people that are important to me.
- *Little finger*: I'm dreaming of.../I dream of...

ID card (Variation 2)

This symbol tells something about me. (Draw something that is meaningful to you.) I have a lot of experience in… I would like to learn to… For me it is very important that… My favourite holiday… My favourite book/film…	**This symbol tells something about me.** (Draw something that is meaningful to you.) I have a lot of experience in… I would like to learn to… For me it is very important that… My favourite holiday… My favourite book/film…
This symbol tells something about me. (Draw something that is meaningful to you.) I have a lot of experience in… I would like to learn to… For me it is very important that… My favourite holiday… My favourite book/film…	**This symbol tells something about me.** (Draw something that is meaningful to you.) I have a lot of experience in… I would like to learn to… For me it is very important that… My favourite holiday… My favourite book/film…

DIVERSITY
Discover the diversity in the group

Risk level: medium

Energy level: medium

Number of participants: 20+

Age: 8+

Time: 5 minutes

Materials: masking tape

Explanation

Divide the space in 4 by making a cross on the ground with masking tape. Ask the participants to stand close to the centre line of the cross.

'All those who have blue and grey eyes go to the left, the others go to the right.

Stay on the same side of the centre line. The boys move into these squares, the girls into those.' (Indicate which squares and the centre line.)

'Look around – what do you notice, what strikes you as obvious?' (Invite comments, thoughts and observations from the group members.)

Repeat the exercise with following categories:

• *Left/right*: people who regularly go to church, mosque or other place of worship/seldom go to a place of worship.

Front/back: live in the city/live in the countryside.

- *Left/right*: play team sports/don't play team sports.

  Front/back: often play computer games/seldom play computer games.

- *Left/right*: are always on time/seldom on time.

  Front/back: wear a watch/don't wear a watch.

Depending on the group, you can create different categories. Some suggestions:

- born in this country/not born in this country
- believe in God/don't believe in God
- live in a family with their parents/don't live with their parents
- have a boyfriend or a girlfriend/are single at the moment
- have their mobile in their pocket/don't have a mobile in their pocket
- like shopping/don't like shopping
- like reading/don't like reading
- would like to travel or live in another country/want to stay in the same country.

Comment

This game can be used as a warm-up for exploring diversity.

When you give the instruction, use body language to show where you want the participants to go. You can also draw the different categories with arrows on a flipchart: this way, participants can see which way they have to move.

Debriefing

- How did you find this activity?
- What surprised you?
- What did it tell you about diversity in our group?
- How did it feel when you were a part of a large group?
- How was it to stand alone?

I AM UNIQUE
Discover the unique members of the group

Risk level: medium
Energy level: medium
Number of participants: 12+
Age: 6+

Time: 5 minutes
Materials: for every 3 participants a simple instrument (cymbals, drum, bell, horn…)

Explanation

Participants sit in a circle. Place the instruments in front of every third participant.

> **'What makes you unique in this group? Are you the only one who goes to ballet lessons, are you the only one who was born abroad? Are you the only one who can play the piano? One after another you are going to complete the sentence "I think I am unique in this circle/group because…" If you share the same experience as the speaker, you pick up the closest instrument and make noise with it.'**

Start by giving an example yourself. Choose something that you think is probably shared by one or 2 participants, for example: 'I think I am unique in this group because I like Mozart's music.'

One after another the participants share their sentence and see if others respond with an instrument.

If the participants like this game (and if the group is not too large) you can do several rounds.

Comment

This game can be used as a warm-up in preparation for exploring diversity. The joy in the game is to be unique. In the setting of diversity, being unique is often a cause of misunderstanding. With this game you can discuss the topic 'Is it fun to be different? Or how do you like to fit in?' or 'What do you need to do to enjoy and have fun when you are together with people who are different?'

Debriefing

- How did you find this activity?
- What surprised you?
- What did you learn from it?

VARIATION

Participants say a sentence which they imagine they share with 2 or 3 participants. They use the sentence: 'I am rare in this group because I...'

TRUTH AND HONOUR
Make a coat of arms

Risk level: medium
Energy level: low
Number of participants: 12–50
Age: 10+

Time: 10 minutes
Materials: copy of blank shields for each participant and lots of coloured markers

Explanation

Participants sit around a table. Download the shield template (see p.71) from www.jkp.com/catalogue/book/9781849051927/resources, print it out and give everyone a copy with coloured pens.

> **'In the Middle Ages knights, or their families, had a coat of arms rich with image and colour. These symbolized the qualities and values they held as important. For example, a lion was often a symbol for courage, and a crane or dog for loyalty. Cities and institutions still have coats of arms today.'**

Use a flipchart to illustrate some ideas on a blank shield:

- My interests.
- What makes me happy?
- What are my strengths?
- What are my dreams and ambitions?

- On a banner, write a quote that describes something about yourself.

  'Now draw your own coat of arms. Use colours and images to express something of yourself and your values. You can also use words or quotes. When everyone is ready we will present what we've done to the group.'

Allow 15 minutes, and when the participants are ready they present their shields.

- In smaller groups they can present their shields to everyone.

- In larger groups it is best to divide the group into groups of 6.

An alternative method is to work in pairs, allowing approximately 2 minutes each to talk about their shield. Then repeat the exercise with 2 different partners.

Comment

This is a high-risk activity as people are disclosing personal aspects of themselves. Working in pairs or small groups helps to alleviate some of the risk. If there is a lot of respect and sensitivity in the group it can be fun to present to the whole group.

Debriefing

- How did you find making the shield?

- How was it to present yourself in this way?

- How did you find hearing others' presentations?

VARIATION

This activity can be used with existing teams as a team-building exercise. Ask the members to fill in a shield with:

- the important values in our team

- the strengths of our team

- the achievements of our team

- what I most like about our team

- the potential or opportunities for our team.

The team can then come up with a collective design for their coat of arms.

Shield template
Fill in the shield with drawings and colours.

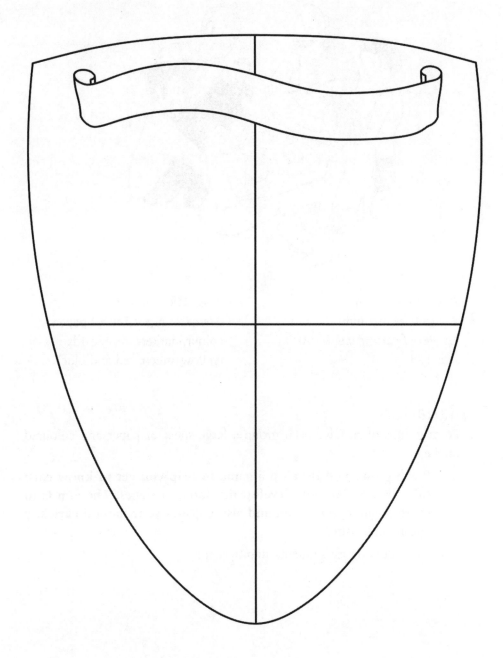

COMMUNITY GAME!
Create a game to help get to know each other better

Risk level: medium

Energy level: medium

Number of participants: 8–50

Age: 12+

Time: 100 minutes

Materials: big sheets of paper,
colour markers, dice, cards
(yellow, green, red and blue)

Explanation

Form groups of 6. Give each group a large sheet of paper and coloured
markers.

> **'Each group will develop a game to help you get to know each
> other better. We will develop the game in stages. The aim is to
> create a game that is fun and also engages your natural curiosity
> about each other.'**

Give the following assignments step by step:

Time	Instruction
5 minutes	**'On your sheet of paper create a board game with 30 squares. Allow yourselves the freedom to create a design that draws on everyone's ideas (see diagram on p.74).'** Draw some examples on a sheet or board, e.g. 'Monopoly', 'Snakes and Ladders', 'Trivial Pursuit'…
10 minutes	**'Each member of a group invents 4 questions or instructions for the game. Write these on coloured cards. Yellow card: an easy question to ask someone, e.g. "What is your favourite sport?" Red card: a tricky question to ask someone, e.g. "What don't you like about yourself?" Green card: an instruction to show something about yourself, e.g. "Sing a nursery rhyme you still remember from your childhood" or "Quote a favourite song or poem." Blue card: something related to the workshop, e.g. "What is your experience with listening and communication skills?" Put all the cards of the same colour face down in separate stacks. On the board, colour 5 squares yellow, 5 green, 5 red and 5 blue, leaving 10 blank.'** (Illustrate your explanation by colouring in some of the squares on your example.) **'When you land on one of the squares you take the corresponding coloured card from the top of the stack, read the question and respond.'**
5 minutes	**'Draw question marks in the 5 blank squares that are left. When you land on these squares someone in the group will ask you a question. Decide who will ask the question, e.g. the person on your left, someone you choose…and discuss what the questions can be about or not.'**
3 minutes	**'Before you begin, go around the group to see if there are any other rules you want to include. Discuss any suggestions and when you have a consensus and everyone is ready, begin.'**
30 minutes	Give each group a die. The participants use a personal object as their counter. **'Play the game and enjoy. You can play until…'**

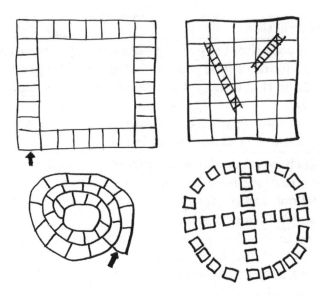

When the time is up, participants sit in a circle for the debriefing.

Comment

This activity is suitable for a group where people know each other to some extent already. The participants define for themselves the depth and subject matter of the exchange, and this often contributes to a positive evaluation of the exercise. You can use the evaluation to define specific group rules for the rest of a workshop or for the period the group stays together.

If the participants are struggling to find the creativity to generate questions and instructions, you can encourage them by giving examples or by preparing some questions and instructions on cards. There are some ideas suggested in Variations 1 and 2 below.

Debriefing

- How did you find playing the game?
- How did you find constructing the game?
- Did the game help you get to know each other better? And if so, what did you learn?
- What did you enjoy in this game? (Ask them to write this on a flipchart.)
- How could this activity be better? (Also take notes of this on a flipchart.)

In a further debriefing you can discuss how the evaluation of this game can inspire some ground rules for the group.

VARIATION 1

Younger groups may lack the creativity to formulate questions and instructions by themselves, in which case you can prepare some cards beforehand. Some ideas for teenagers:

- What is your favourite colour?
- What is your favourite pet?
- Who do you admire?
- What is your favourite food?
- What is your favourite TV programme?
- What are your hobbies and interests?
- What things do you dislike?
- What would you do with £10,000? (Select appropriate currency.)
- What are you scared of?
- What do you like about yourself?
- What is the best book you have ever read?
- What is your favourite music?
- What would you never do again? What do you regret?
- What quality do you most like in a friend?
- What would you do again if you could?
- Are you addicted to anything, and if so what?
- What is your first memory?
- What do you like doing during the holidays?
- What are your favourite things about school?
- What do your friends like about you?
- What would you like to be doing in 10 years?
- Hum your favourite song.
- Imitate someone you like and let the others guess who it is.
- Pantomime your favourite animal.
- Tell a joke.
- Can you click your heels in the air?

With these suggestions teenagers usually access their own creativity, so keep some cards blank for their ideas.

VARIATION 2

This game can be adapted for a specific workshop. For example, for a parents' evening about 'Educating youngsters' you can write these questions on a board game:

- What do I like about my daughter/son?
- What are my concerns when I think about teenagers?
- When I think about educating my child what are my concerns?
- When I see my kid am I reminded of anything about my own teenage years, and if so what?
- How does my child deal with our family rules?
- What do I think contributes to self-esteem in teenagers?
- If they lose touch with their own self-worth, what can contribute to regaining it?
- What is fun and enjoyable to do with teenagers?
- How do I respond when I judge my child has made a mistake?
- Who supports me in my role as a parent?
- How much money does my child get per month?
- How might you discuss serious issues such as drugs with your child?
- How do I discuss sex and relationships with my child?
- What quality or value would I like to pass on to my child?
- Did I make good choices as a teenager? If so, then what helped? If not, what would have helped?
- What did I need when I was 14?
- Recalling my teenage years, what things do I still recall and appreciate about the adults who contributed to me, if anything?
- What mistakes did I make when I was a teenager?
- Recalling my teenage years, if I could do some things differently, what would they be?
- If I could express some gratitude from my teenage years, to whom would it be and what would I say?

- What helped me make good choices when I was young?

- Recalling my youth, what do I like about my parents or those adults who cared for me?

- What, if anything, do I do differently with my kids compared to my parents?

PRESS MEETING
Interviewing as community building

Risk level: medium
Energy level: medium
Number of participants: 8–20
Age: 10+

Time: 30 minutes
Materials: copy of the press
questionnaire, pencils

Explanation

Download the press questionnaire (see p.80) from www.jkp.com/catalogue/book/9781849051927/resources, make 3 copies for each participant and hand them out with some pencils.

> **'You are press reporters. Interview at least one person and ensure that you are also interviewed at least once. You can use the questionnaire as a guide or you can invent your own questions.'**

Allow 15 minutes for this and then come together in a circle.

> **'Now I want you to present someone else, using your notes. Only include the things that impressed you.'**

After someone has been presented, allow them to respond, add or correct anything that was said. Ensure that everyone is presented and also allow for people to present more than one person, or for one person to be presented by 2 different people.

Comment

This is a medium-risk activity which can help create more of a sense of openness in a serious or cautious group. It is good to co-ordinate the end of the interviews using a bell or a gong.

Debriefing

- What was it like to be interviewed?
- How did you find being the reporter?
- Which role did you prefer and why?
- How was it to present someone to the group?
- How was it to be presented to the group?
- Does this activity contribute to a sense of community or team building and if so, how?

Press questionnaire

Name of the interviewee
Who is your favourite musician?
What is your favourite book or film?
What is your favourite ever holiday?
What would be your motto?
When and where are you happiest?
How do you relax?
Which living person do you most admire, and why?
If you could edit your past, what would you change?
If you could travel back in time, where would you go?
What makes you cry and when was the last time you cried?
Cat or dog?
What is your guiltiest pleasure?
If you won the lottery, what would you do with the money?
If you were an animal, what would you be?
What is your most used word or phrase?
Which people, living or dead, would you invite to a dinner party?
What are you afraid of?
Who would you like to say sorry to and why?
What single thing would most enhance the quality of your life?
If you could wake up tomorrow with a new skill or talent, what would you choose?

 downloadable

BINGO
Bingo game to stimulate contact

Risk level: medium

Energy level: medium

Number of participants: 10–50

Age: 8+

Time: 10 minutes

Materials: bingo cards, 'peer bingo' cards, 'autograph' cards

Explanation

Participants sit in a circle.

Give each participant a bingo card. (Download the template at www.jkp.com/catalogue/book/9781849051927/resources and print.)

> **'On the card there are a variety of statements about people. The aim is to find people that these statements are true for. When you do find someone then write their name in the box. When you have filled 5 connecting boxes you shout "Bingo!" If there is still time left you can start on another row. You have 7 minutes. Go!'**

Stop the game after 7 minutes.

Comment

This is a quick, easy icebreaker. When you give the instructions make sure you focus on having fun and getting to know people, rather than on winning.

Debriefing

Ask how many 'Bingos' the participants had.

- How did you find the game?
- Did you have a strategy?
- What did you learn about other members of the group?

VARIATION 1

Give each person a 'Peer Bingo' card. (Download the template at www.jkp. com/catalogue/book/9781849051927/resources and print.) Everyone fills this in with their own preferences and, once everyone has done this, they look for others who have the same preferences. Each time they find someone they fill in that person's name. When they have 4 connected boxes, they shout 'Bingo!'

VARIATION 2: COLLECT AUTOGRAPHS

Give every participant a copy of the sheet 'Autographs'. (Download the template at www.jkp.com/catalogue/book/9781849051927/resources and print.) The goal is for participants to find someone to sign in every box. At the end, evaluate which boxes aren't filled.

This variant is less hilarious but it also stimulates contact with several people.

Bingo

Write in each box the name of the person for whom these statements are true.

Has a pet	Plays a musical instrument	Loves to sleep late	Plays sport	Speaks 3 languages
Has brothers or sisters	Has lived abroad	Regularly reads books	Regularly goes to the cinema	Is good at drawing
Can change a car tyre	Is good at maths	Frequently uses public transport	Can swim a kilometre/mile	Is/was in the Scouts
Is a good cook	Can skate	Is a strong swimmer	Has a favourite pastime	Has travelled abroad
Enjoys dancing	Has children	Can skateboard	Has a garden	Has done a martial art

Peer bingo

Write your preferences in each box, then find others who share them.

Favourite pet:	Favourite music:	Favourite TV programme:	Favourite colour:
Birthday month:	City/village where I live:	Favourite food:	I am scared of:
Favourite book/ movie:	Subject I like(d) at school:	Favourite holiday place:	Favourite drink:
Shoe size:	Tree or flower I like:	Favourite wild animal:	What gives me energy:

Autographs

Find someone to sign up for each of the boxes and add the additional information.

Plays a musical instrument. What do you play?	Has a sister. What is her name?	Likes to sleep in a tent. When and where was the last time?
Has drawing skills. When did you last make a drawing?	Has a pet. What pet?	Plays sport. What sport?
Likes to sing. Favourite song?	Likes reading. What was the book you last read?	Spends more than 3 hours each week pursuing a hobby. What hobby?
Likes computer games. What is your favourite?	Likes travelling. What is your favourite place?	Likes films. What is your favourite film?

GRAPHOLOGY
Present yourself in a written form

Risk level: medium
Energy level: low
Number of participants: 8–20

Age: 10+
Time: 30–60 minutes
Materials: paper, pencils, colours

Explanation

Participants sit in a circle. Give everyone a sheet, a pencil and coloured markers.

> **'On your paper I want you to try to give a sense of yourself using drawings and words. Ideas of things you might include are:**
>
> - **what your interests are**
> - **what your strengths are**
> - **what you appreciate in other people**
> - **what you would like to get from this workshop.**
>
> **Feel free to write and draw however you like but don't include your name, as I would like us all to try to guess whose sheet belongs to whom. You have 5 minutes.'**

Pin up the sheets when everyone is ready and discuss each sheet in turn.

> **'What catches your attention when you look at this sheet? What does the handwriting say about this person? When you look at the layout of the sheet, what impression do you have?'**

Participants then try to guess who created the sheet. When several people have tried to guess, reveal the person who made it and allow them to add information or respond to the observations of the group if they wish to. Divide the time equally among the sheets, allowing 2 minutes per sheet.

Comment

Allow a maximum of 7 minutes to make the sheets. Ensure that the analysis time is divided equally between the sheets (suggested maximum of 2 minutes per sheet).

Debriefing

- How was it to present yourself in this way?
- How did you find the analysis of the sheets?

I AM, I WAS, I HAVE
Find similarities with others in the group

Risk level: medium
Energy level: medium
Number of participants: 6–12
Age: 12+

Time: 10 minutes
Materials: 1 copy per person of the form, pencils

Explanation

Participants sit in a circle at a table. Give each participant a copy of the sheet on p.90 (download at www.jkp.com/catalogue/book/9781849051927/resources and print) and a pencil.

> **'The goal is to write on your sheet characteristics, qualities or interests you have in common with others in the group. How? One at a time a person says a sentence that starts with: "I am…" or "I like…" or "I have …" For example, "I have a bike." People who have a bike raise their hands.**
>
> **Count how many other people have a bike and if, for example, 4 people have a bike, then they all write "have a bike" in the box for something they have in common with 4 other people in the group. Repeat the process for each person. The aim is to fill all the boxes.'**

Play the game until a number of people have completed their sheet.

Comment

This game is excellent for smaller groups and for people who are not ready to engage in more high-risk or playful activities.

Debriefing

- How did you find this game?
- Did this exercise help you get to know the others in your group? And if so, how?
- What else would you like to know about the others?

I am, I was, I have

Write in the grid the things you have in common with others in the group.

Name: . . . .

This is something unique to me in this group.	This is something I have in common with **1** person in this group.
This is something I have in common with **2** people in this group.	This is something I have in common with **3** people in this group.
This is something I have in common with **4** people in this group.	This is something I have in common with **5** people in this group.
This is something I have in common with **6** people in this group.	This is something I have in common with **7** people in this group.
This is something I have in common with **8** people in this group.	This is something I have in common with **9** people in this group.
This is something I have in common with **10** people in this group.	This is something I have in common with **11** people in this group.

 downloadable

WHAT IS YOUR OPINION?

Group members indicate their opinion by standing either side of a line

Risk level: medium–high
Energy level: low
Number of participants: 12–30

Age: 8+
Time: 10 minutes
Materials: masking tape

Explanation

Make a line on the floor with masking tape and write 'agree' on one side and 'disagree' on the other.

Ask the participants to straddle the line (see picture).

'Close your eyes. I will make a statement and you must decide whether you agree or disagree with it. I will count to 3, and on "3" step to one side or the other before opening your eyes.'

Ideas for statements

- Chocolate gives you energy.
- Pets make you happy.
- Money makes you happy.
- It is more fun to play sport than to watch.

- Sport helps you live longer.
- Children should always obey their parents.
- Unemployed people are lazy.
- It is important that we look after the environment.
- Women make better leaders than men.

After each statement ask if anyone wants to say why they made their particular choice.

Comment

A good activity to start a workshop/lesson around a specific subject. It encourages some reflection on an issue without initially having to explain one's opinion.

Debriefing

- Which choices were easy to make?
- Were there any difficult choices? And if so, what?
- How do you feel about others having a different opinion?

VARIATION

Make a line on the floor. At the one end place a card with the word 'agree' and at the other end 'disagree'. Read different statements and ask the participants to stand somewhere on the line indicating the strength of their agreement or disagreement with the statement.

This variation gives participants the opportunity to show a nuance in their choice. During the process you might ask if anyone would like to comment on their choice and whether they were influenced by the choices of others.

I HEAR AND FEEL YOU
Community building with sound and physical contact

Risk level: medium–high
Energy level: medium
Number of participants: 8–30

Age: 10+
Time: 10+
Materials: none

Explanation

Form groups of 10 people, each group standing in a circle.

> **'In the first round we are going to get to know each other by the sound of our voices. Close your eyes and keep them closed until I let you know when to open them.**
>
> **In turn each person says "My name is…"**
>
> **Listen carefully to the sound of each person's voice and try to remember their name.'**

Each participant says their name.

> **'Now, keeping your eyes closed, carefully move to another place in the circle.'**

Participants change places.

> **'Now open your eyes and look around. In turn each person says where they live, and the rest of the group tries to guess their name.**
>
> **Now the second round.'**

The participants stay in the same circles.

> 'I want you to move around your circle and shake each person's hand and both say your names. Try to recall the name and the handshake. When everyone has finished, form a circle again.
>
> Now, taking it in turns, stand in the middle with your eyes closed. A few people come forward, shake your hand and you have to try to guess who they are from their handshake.'

Comment

This energizer is a good way to start a workshop related to the importance of using all your senses for learning, listening and communicating.

Debriefing

- How did you find this activity?
- Did it contribute to community building and if so, how?
- How hard or easy did you find it to recognize someone by their voice?
- What characteristics can you connect with the voice?
- How was it to recognize someone by a handshake?
- What, if anything, do you get a sense of from someone from their handshake?

NAME SMASH

Learning names in a reaction game

Risk level: high

Energy level: high

Number of participants: 12–30

Age: 6+

Time: 10 minutes

Materials: a newspaper or 'boffer'

Explanation

Participants sit in a circle on the ground with their legs extended into the centre. One person stands in the middle with a loosely rolled up newspaper.

> **'The person in the middle is the smasher and has to try to hit people's feet. He can only hit the feet of someone when their name is called out, but if they call someone else's name before they have been hit then they are safe. Are you ready? The person I point to is to start.'**

This person must call someone else's name, and so on. If the smasher manages to hit someone, they then become the smasher in the middle.

After a while add the following rule:

> **'When your name is called a further 3 times you can cross your legs; you are then smash-proof and your name can't be called.'**

The introduction of this rule gradually brings the game to an end as one by one the participants cross their legs.

Comment

This is a fun name game.

Initially practise the rules of the game in slow motion so that everyone understands them.

VARIATION

The group stands in a circle shoulder to shoulder with their fists held out. The smasher stands in the middle trying to whack people's hands when their name is called.

THAT IS RIGHT BUT...

Guess what others think about you

Risk level: high
Energy level: low
Number of participants: 12–50
Age: 10+

Time: 10 minutes
Materials: chairs for each person, plus 1 extra chair

Explanation

Participants sit in a circle. There is one 'friends chair' which is empty.

> **'Consider qualities you have that you think your friends appreciate about you. Pick one of these qualities that is important to you, for example: "Others like to be my friend because I am a good listener."'**

Allow a minute for people to choose.

> **'So one person sits on the "friends chair" and the rest of the group try to guess the quality that person has chosen, starting with a sentence like: "I think people like to be your friend because..."**
>
> **The person on the chair can respond in 3 ways.**
>
> - **Thank you, but that is not what I was thinking of.**
>
> - **Thank you, that is not something I think of about myself.**
>
> - **Thank you. That is what I was thinking about.'**

The group has 10 guesses. If they haven't guessed after 10 then the person in the 'friends chair' reveals the quality they had in mind. Then another person sits in the 'friends chair'.

Participants get only one chance in the 'friends chair'. The game is over when everyone who wishes to has sat in the 'friends chair'.

Comment

This is a high-risk activity with participants disclosing ideas about themselves in a group. They also receive feedback from their fellow group members.

Debriefing

- How did you find choosing a sentence for yourself?
- How did you find sitting hearing people's guesses?
- Did you learn anything from playing this game and if so, what?
- Do you have any ideas for variations of this game that you would find interesting and if so, what?

VARIATION

You can use other sentences. Some examples:

- People want to go on holiday with me because...
- People will remember me because...
- People recognize me in the street because...

You can have the group say what they most appreciate about the person in the 'friends chair'.

You can have the group say the person in the 'friends chair' would be 'the first person I would ask to play chess with' or 'the first person I would ask to help me with my maths'. Or the person in the 'friends chair' would be the first person to say '...did you see the football' or '...it was great'. Or the person in the 'friends chair' would be the first person to be a business man, or a lawyer, or a doctor, or a teacher, etc

FIRST IMPRESSION

Check if your first impression matches with reality

Risk level: high
Energy level: low
Number of participants: 12–30
Age: 12+

Time: 20 minutes
Materials: 3 copies of the form per person, pencils

Explanation

Participants sit in a double circle facing a random partner.

Give everyone one copy of the form on p.101 to fill in (download at www.jkp.com/catalogue/book/9781849051927/resources and print) and a pencil.

> **'Look at your partner and consider what this person is like and how this person lives. Then fill in the form. When you are both ready, share your perceptions and see if your assumptions were close or miles off target.'**

Allow 6 minutes and then everyone moves 2 places to the left and repeats the procedure. Then repeat a third time.

Comment

A good exercise for self-exploration.

Debriefing

- How accurate do you think your first impressions are?
- Did you learn anything about yourself? And if so, what?
- Did you learn anything about others? And if so, what?

First impression

My first impression of: . . . .

Circle what you think about your partner.

- *This person lives* in the city – in a suburb – in the countryside – in a fancy apartment – [something else]
- *This person loves* the sea – the mountains – staying home – shopping – [something else]
- *This person lives* alone – in a family – in a commune – with friends – with a partner – [none of these]
- *This person believes in* Jesus – Islam – the Buddha – UFOs – money – is a non-believer.
- *This person likes* dogs – cats – other pets – no pets.

I think that this person has the following:

- *interests*. . . . .
- *characteristics* shy – adventurous – calm – generous – intelligent – curious – playful – determined – easy-going – [other]
- *talents* artistic – sporting – organized – computer skills – creative – leadership – [other]

I think this person:

- likes to . . . .
- hates to . . . .
- is very special because. . . . .

CAN I ASK YOU SOMETHING?
In-depth interview

Risk level: high

Energy level: low

Number of participants: 4–12

Age: 11+

Time: 20+ minutes

Materials: sheets of paper, pencils

Explanation

Participants sit around a table with a sheet of paper each.

> **'Write your name on the top of your paper and pass it to the right. What would you like to know about this person? Write your question on the sheet and then pass it to the right.**
>
> **Only write respectful questions and avoid questions with a "yes-or-no" answer. A good structure for open questions might start with "How...", "What do you...", "What is important...", "What is your..."**
>
> **Keep passing the sheets around and writing questions until you get your own sheet back.'**

Once everyone has their own sheet back, the participants stand in a circle. Each person in turn reads a question they have been asked and which they would like to answer. Continue around the circle until everyone has had a go. Depending on the time allowed you could do several rounds. There is no need to answer all the questions.

You can change the energy of the group by asking them to stand when they have got their own sheets back; or when it is their turn they stand to read and answer the question. Staying seated makes the exercise slightly lower risk.

Comment

This activity is useful for people who already know each other. Depending on the skill, awareness and atmosphere within the group, you might consider allowing follow-up questions to facilitate a deeper, more personal exchange between the participants.

Debriefing

- What was it like composing your questions?
- How was it to respond?
- What kinds of questions were most useful for this kind or activity?
- What was the most interesting aspect of this exercise and why?

FORMING SUBGROUPS

Small groups help the participants feel safe and allow for more lively interaction, especially when you want the group to explore or share more personal feelings and ideas.

Regularly changing the formation of the small groups in a random manner enables the participants to have a broader personal interaction. This contributes to team building in the larger group.

An important element in making groups is that it is done randomly. An easy way to do this is to ask the participants to 'number off' 1 to 4 around the whole group. The groups are formed of people with the same number. This chapter suggests a number of more creative ways of randomly forming groups to enhance the participants' enjoyment and fun, which in turn contributes to a sense of belonging and team building.

Some of the games in this chapter, as well as being a fun way of mixing the group up, have more potential. With these games we suggest some debriefing questions.

1, 2, 3, 4

Risk level: low
Energy level: medium
Number of participants: 8–50
Age: 8+

Time: 5 minutes
Materials: cards with numbers
1–4, enough for 1 for each
participant

Explanation

Prepare cards numbered 1 to 4, enough for one card per person. Everyone takes a card and remembers their number.

> **'I want you to form groups with others who have the same number as you, but you are not allowed to talk or signal. You may only shake hands, feeling if the other person is the same number as yourself.'**

The participants start shaking hands and form groups with those who 'shake' the same way.

PUZZLE

Risk level: low
Energy level: medium
Number of participants: 8–50

Age: 8+
Time: 5 minutes
Materials: postcards cut into 4

Explanation

To form groups, take 4 postcards and cut them into 4 pieces, giving each participant a piece of postcard.

> **'I want you to form groups with others who have the other pieces of the same postcard. No talking. When you have found the others, sit in a circle and assemble the postcard puzzle.'**

The objective is to form groups with those people who have a piece of the same postcard.

ROPES FOR PAIRS

Risk level: low
Energy level: medium
Number of participants: 8–60
Age: 8+

Time: 5 minutes
Materials: 1 rope for each 2 participants

Explanation

Prepare ropes of approximately 2 metres in length and about 6mm diameter, one rope for every 2 participants. Hold the ropes in the middle (see picture), so no one can see which end connects to any other.

> **'Everyone take an end of the rope, and without letting go of the rope, pair up with the person at the other end.'**

VARIATION

To form groups of 4, tie ropes in pairs in the middle.

FORMING PAIRS

Risk level: low
Energy level: medium
Number of participants: 8–60
Age: 8+

Time: 5–10 minutes
Materials: card, and tape to stick
the card to people's backs

Explanation

Download the template on the following page from www.jkp.com/catalogue/book/9781849051927/resources, print a copy, cut out the words and give each participant a card, ensuring that each is part of a pair. Ask them to stick their card on someone's back.

'You have a word on your back that forms a pair with another word. Your goal is to find the person who has the matching word on their back asking only yes-or-no questions to each other. When you have found your partner, stay together and help others if asked.'

VARIATION 1

Instead of asking questions, participants are allowed only to mime.

VARIATION 2

With a more informal group you can stick the cards on the forehead. Cigarette paper, on which you have written the words beforehand, works well. Make a copy, cut out the words and give each participant a card.

Forming pairs

man	woman
hot	cold
bride	groom
father	mother
dry	wet
sun	moon
black	white
winter	summer
short	long
thunder	lightning
thick	thin
cat	mouse
slow	fast
morning	evening
fox	rabbit

 downloadable

GREETING THE WORLD

Risk level: low
Energy level: medium
Number of participants: 8–60
Age: 8+

Time: 5 minutes
Materials: cards printed from downloadable template on the next page

Explanation

Download the template on the following page from www.jkp.com/catalogue/book/9781849051927/resources, print a copy, cut out the cards, and give each participant a card. You can prepare 2, 3 or more copies of each card, depending on the size of groups you want.

> '**Memorize the word on your card and greet each other with the greeting on your card. Form groups with people who have the same greeting.**'

Greeting the world

Guden taak (Germany)	Bon jour (France)
Bwenos dias (Spain)	Ni hao (China)
Namaste (India)	Bon journow (Italy)
Dobri djeen (Russia)	Djambo (Swaziland)
Djin dobre (Czech Republic)	Ohajoo gozajmas (Japan)
Goodn daaigan (Iceland)	Kalimeera (Greece)
Shalom (Hebrew)	Merhabaa (Arabic/Turkey)
Hiva apai vaa (Finland)	Bom dia (Portugal)

downloadable

RATTLE BOX

Risk level: low
Energy level: medium
Number of participants: 8–60
Age: 8+
Time: 5 minutes

Materials: small boxes of the same size, 1 for each participant, and materials such as rice, small coins, dried beans, stones, etc. to turn the boxes into rattles

Explanation

Prepare small boxes of the same size, for example empty match boxes, one for each participant.

Fill the boxes with different materials, such as rice, stones, beans, salt, nothing… Put the same thing in a number of 'rattle boxes', depending on the size of groups you want. For example, if you want groups of 4, then put rice in 4 boxes, stones in 4, and so on.

Give each participant a box.

'Shake your box, listening for others who you think have the same kind of rattle as yourself, and form into groups with them.'

HUMMING SONGS

Risk level: low
Energy level: medium
Number of participants: 8–60
Age: 8+

Time: 5 minutes
Materials: cards with nursery rhymes written on them, 1 for each participant

Explanation

Prepare cards with the titles of well known nursery rhymes, using a maximum of 5 different songs. Shuffle the cards and give each participant a card that only they can see.

> **'I want you to memorize what's on the card and put it away. Then start humming the nursery rhyme and find others humming the same tune.'**

When the groups are formed you can invite them to make a mime so that the other groups can guess what the song is about.

This game is a good warm-up for a playful group activity.

FORM GROUPS WITH BELONGINGS

Quick, unusual way of forming groups

Risk level: medium
Energy level: medium
Number of participants: 6–30

Age: 6+
Time: 5 minutes
Materials: none

Explanation

The participants sit in a circle.

Ask everyone to put one personal object in the middle of the circle, then, using these belongings, form groups of the size that you want.

'Form groups of…with the people who have their object lying next to yours.'

Comment

In a playful setting you can ask participants to place their left shoe in the middle. For more serious groups it is wiser to use something like a pen.

GROUPING WITH FEELINGS

Risk level: medium
Energy level: medium
Number of participants: 8–60

Age: 8+
Time: 5–10 minutes
Materials: feeling cards

Explanation

Download the template on the next page from www.jkp.com/catalogue/book/9781849051927/resources, print and cut out the cards. You can prepare 2, 3 or more copies of each card, depending on the size of groups you want. The easier cards are in the upper rows.

Shuffle the cards and give the participants one each, making sure that no one else sees their card.

> **'I want you to memorize the word on your card and then put the card away. Use body language to communicate the word that is on your card and form groups of people who express the same feeling.'**

Comment

Use simple words for younger participants.

This energizer can be a warm-up for a session about emotions. As a short debriefing you can ask:

- How was it to mime the word on your card?

- What do you think were the other words?

Grouping with feelings

happy	sad	scared
angry	tired	nervous
frustrated	lonely	relaxed
embarrassed	in love	excited
jealous	curious	annoyed

WHAT IS ON MY BACK?
Form random groups

Risk level: medium
Energy level: medium
Number of participants: 6–50

Age: 10+
Time: 5 minutes
Materials: cards, tape

Explanation

Prepare a set of card pairs, such that each card has a relationship with at least one other. (See examples on the following page.)

Make a stack of these cards and shuffle them, then give each participant a card and some tape.

> **'Stick your card on someone's back. Then form pairs (or groups of 3 or 4) with someone who has a word that relates to your word.'**

Decide in which way participants can help each other, for example:

- no talking allowed, only mime
- participants can only ask yes-or-no questions.

If you want to form pairs, create paired cards such as those on the next page (downloadable from www.jkp.com/catalogue/book/9781849051927/resources).

What is on my back?

Try these:

Barack	Obama
Nelson	Mandela
David	Beckham
John	Lennon
Winston	Churchill

Or these:

day	night
sun	moon
brother	sister
fire	water
cat	mouse

What is on my back?

If you want to form groups of 3:

goat	cow	sheep
green	blue	yellow
one	two	three
Venus	Mars	Jupiter

If you want to form groups of 4:

north	west	east	south
water	fire	earth	air
socks	shoes	hat	shirt
brown	black	yellow	green

SPOT ON THE FOREHEAD

Forming groups of different colours by using colour points on foreheads

Risk level: medium
Energy level: medium
Number of participants: 12–50
Age: 6+

Time: 5 minutes
Materials: adhesive paper, coloured pens, coloured sticky dots

Explanation

Either buy or make some coloured sticky dots (obtainable from office suppliers). The number of colours determines the *size of the groups*, and the number of stickers of the same colour determines the *number of groups*, for example 4 red, 4 green, 4 blue, 4 yellow, 4 brown and 4 purple would create 4 groups of 6 people.

Participants stand in a circle.

Put the stickers on a plate in the middle.

> **'Each person takes a sticker. When everyone is ready, stick your sticker on someone else's forehead, making sure they don't see what colour it is.'**

The participants now stand in a circle, each with a coloured sticker on their forehead.

'In silence, form groups of X [group size] so that every group contains just one of each of the different colours.'

When the groups are formed, everyone can stick their colour on their name badge.

Comment

In the next group activity, you could use the different colours to define specific roles for the work in the groups.

Debriefing

- How was it to form groups without speaking?
- What strategies were used to form groups?

MANGO MANGO
Hilarious group former

Risk level: medium–high
Energy level: high
Number of participants: 12–50
Age: 6+

Time: 5 minutes
Materials: play cards (download and print 2-page template)

Explanation

Download and prepare a set of cards from the templates on pp.125–6, one card per participant. The number of family members will be the *group size* and the number of fruits will be the *number of groups* you end up with.

Participants sit in a circle on *strong* chairs. Shuffle the cards and give each participant a card.

'Your card tells you the name of your family (the fruit) and who you are in this family. When I say "Mango mango" you find the other family members and, as quickly as possible, sit in the correct order.

So, for example, grandfather apple sits with his legs together on the chair. On the lap of grandfather apple sits grandmother apple. Father apple sits on her lap, then mother apple, son apple, daughter apple, and finally, on the daughter's lap sits baby apple.

> **When the whole family is seated they proudly shout: "Mango mango!"'**

Check if all participants have understood and begin by calling 'Mango mango!'

> **'Now, for a second round, stand up and quickly swap cards with everyone else.'**

After 10 seconds or so start the next round by calling 'Mango mango!'

You can repeat this game a few times. In the last round the groups stay together for a group assignment.

Comment

When you explain this, demonstrate that people must sit with their knees together to make their lap as large as possible. This also contributes to the safety of the game.

This activity usually generates a lot of fun and also a lot of noise, so be conscious of other people in the building!

As this is a high-risk contact game, participants may wish to observe rather than play. After the explanation ask if anyone would like to sit out, in which case you will need to hold on to some of the 'babies' cards. Invite the people who pass to take up the role of controller to see which family is first.

Debriefing

- How did you find this activity?
- How was it to sit on someone's lap?
- How was it when you were sitting on the chair with everyone else on top of you?

VARIATION

This is the same exercise, except that instead of shouting, participants have to find their 'family' using mime and body language. A group that is ready whispers 'Mango mango'.

Mango mango

Make a set of cards.
Number of families = number of groups.
Number of family members = size of the groups.

grandfather apple	grandfather banana
grandmother apple	grandmother banana
father apple	father banana
mother apple	mother banana
son apple	son banana
daughter apple	daughter banana
baby apple	baby banana
great-grandfather apple	great-grandfather banana
great-grandmother apple	great-grandmother banana

 downloadable

Mango mango

grandfather tomato	grandfather coconut
grandmother tomato	grandmother coconut
father tomato	father coconut
mother tomato	mother coconut
son tomato	son coconut
daughter tomato	daughter coconut
baby tomato	baby coconut
great-grandfather tomato	great-grandfather coconut
great-grandmother tomato	great-grandmother coconut

 downloadable

TWO FEET, ONE HAND
Forming groups using creativity and teamwork

Risk level: high

Energy level: high

Number of participants: 12–50

Age: 6+

Time: 10 minutes

Material: whistle or gong

Explanation

Instruct everyone to walk quickly around the room using all the space, but to avoid touching anyone.

> **'When I ring the gong, form groups according to the number of gongs. So if I hit the gong 4 times, then form groups of 4. If you don't find a group, stand aside and observe until the next round.**
>
> **Each group has 10 seconds to stand on 4 hands and 4 feet, making sure nothing else touches the ground.'**

Notice which groups successfully completed the task.

Then once again, everyone walks around the room.

Repeat the exercise, forming groups according to the number of gongs. Each time give them a task with a time restriction; for example:

- groups of *3*: stand on 2 feet

- groups of *6*: stand on 2 feet and 2 hands

- groups of *5*: no feet touching the ground

- groups of 7: bring all feet higher than all the heads
  - groups of 6: all heads lower than all hands
  - groups of 5: only hands touching the ground
  - groups of 4: without touching anything on the ground.

(With luck one of the groups will find out that a simultaneous jump fulfils the instruction for a moment.)

Comment

The time restriction encourages creative solutions and maximum participation. The last 3 assignments can work for a group of any size.

VARIATION 1

You can broaden out the body parts in contact with the ground, for example, 1 foot, 2 elbows, a tummy, a hand and a bum.

VARIATION 2

You can challenge the groups to see which team can reach furthest across the room with all team members remaining in contact with each other but only certain body parts touching the ground – for example, with a group of 8, 1 back, 1 foot, 3 hands, a knee, 2 bums, 1 tummy and an elbow. You might list the body parts on a card to help them remember.

DISCO
Form groups dancing

Risk level: high
Energy level: high
Number of participants: 8–60

Age: 8+
Time: 5 minutes
Materials: disco cards

Explanation

Download, print and cut out the cards from the template on the next page (www.jkp.com/catalogue/book/9781849051927/resources). You can prepare 2, 3 or more copies of each card, depending on the size of groups you want.

Give each participant a card.

> **'I want you to memorize what is on your card and put it away. Without speaking, find other people to form a group who have the same dance as yourself.'**

Disco cards

waltz	salsa
disco	flamenco
slow	jive

FLIRTING

Change places with someone who winks at you

Risk level: high
Energy level: high
Number of participants: 6–30
Age: 6+

Time: 10 minutes
Materials: chairs or cushions, 1 for all but 1 of the participants

Explanation

Participants sit in a circle with one person in the middle.

> '**I want you to look around the circle, catch someone's eye and wink at them. Then they wink back. When you have both winked, you both leave your seats and try to change places. The person in the middle tries to sit in an empty chair, leaving a new person in the middle.**
>
> **Each of you must change places at least 3 times during the game, but when you've changed places 6 times you don't return anyone's wink.**'

Having mixed the circle up, divide them into the size of groups you need.

Comment

This game mixes up the group as people exchange eye contact: they will sit next to a number of different people, generating energy and fun. When you divide groups in this way they readily accept the fairness inherent in the random manner of forming the groups.

Debriefing

- How was it to play this game?
- What did you enjoy?
- Which role did you prefer?
- How was it to wink at people?

VARIATION 1

Divide the group roughly in 2. Now form a circle of chairs so that one group member is standing *behind* each chair and the other group members sit *on* a chair; leave 3 empty chairs.

The players behind the empty chairs entice someone seated on another chair by winking at them. When a player on a chair is winked at, they must quickly try to escape to the empty chair of the person who winked at them. However, the person standing behind your chair must try to stop you escaping by holding you by the shoulders.

The guards standing behind the chairs must keep their hands behind their backs until the person in their chair has been winked at.

After some time change roles so that the seated people now act as the guards, and vice versa.

COMMENT

Teenagers like this game because it is a safe way to explore looking at and being looked at – an important aspect of making contact with others.

VARIATION 2

Having made smaller groups you can play the same game with the smaller numbers.

HURRICANE
Change places with the wind

Risk level: medium–high
Energy level: high
Number of participants: 15–50
Age: 6+

Time: 10 minutes
Materials: chairs, 1 for each participant

Explanation

Participants sit in a circle of chairs and you stand in the middle.

> 'The person in the middle says the following phrase, adding some names of other participants. For example: "The wind blows for Jack, Emilia and Elena and everyone who is wearing socks."
>
> If your name is called out, or if you are included in the extra distinction, in this case you are wearing socks, then you have to change places quickly. The person in the middle also tries to grab a seat.'

Practise this game a few times using both visible and invisible characteristics, for example people who wear black shoes (visible), people who like chocolate (invisible).

When everyone has grasped the idea of the game you can add the refinement that if the person in the middle says 'Hurricane!' then everyone has to change chairs. The last person standing starts the game afresh.

By the time you have played for a few minutes, most people will have changed places and be sitting next to different people. Divide the circle in parts to form subgroups for the next activity.

Comment

This game lifts the energy of the group and helps divide the group randomly, which participants readily accept.

Debriefing

- How was it to play this game?
- What did you enjoy?
- How was it to stand in the middle?
- What makes this game so funny?

VARIATION

You can vary the opening instruction with:

'I know John, Emilia, Elena and I would like to get to know all people who...'

This variant is a favourite for teenagers because they like to say who they know.

I SIT IN THE GRASS
A playful, structured place-changing game

Risk level: high
Energy level: high
Number of participants: 15–50
Age: 6+

Time: 10 minutes
Materials: chairs for all
participants, plus 1 extra chair

Explanation

Participants sit in a circle of chairs with one extra chair empty. You stand in the middle.

'The person who sits to the left of the empty chair starts by patting the empty chair and says: "I sit", and sits on the empty chair.

The next person, now to the left of the new empty chair, pats the empty chair and says: "in the grass", and sits on the empty chair.

The next person, to the left of the new empty chair, pats the chair and says: "and I like..." and you name someone from the group, then you sit on the empty chair.

The person whose name is called gets up and sits on the empty chair, and then the person who sits to the left of the new empty chair repeats the first step: "I sit."'

Practise this for a few rounds until everyone understands the game, then add another rule:

> **'Now the person in the middle tries to sit on an empty chair before it is claimed. As soon as the person on the left of an empty chair has patted it, and claimed it, that chair is no longer available. Also, the chair for the person whose name is called cannot be taken, but the chair they have vacated is up for grabs. If you lose your chair, then you go into the middle, the game begins again and you try to sit in an empty chair.'**

By the time you have played for a while, most people will have changed places and will be sitting next to different people. You can then divide the circle in parts to form subgroups for the next activity.

Comment

This game lifts the energy and meets needs for play and structure. When you divide groups in this way they readily accept the fairness inherent in the random manner of forming the groups.

Debriefing

- How was it to play this game?
- What did you enjoy?
- How was it when someone said 'and I like…' about you?

THE WAVE
Energetic activity, frequently changing places

Risk level: high
Energy level: high
Number of participants: 12–60
Age: 6+

Time: 10 minutes
Materials: chairs for all
participants, plus 1 extra chair

Explanation

The participants sit in a circle of chairs with one chair empty. You stand in the middle to explain the game and steer the waves.

> **'There are 4 different waves we will try.**
>
> **First the "left wave". So when you have an empty chair on your left side, you stand up and drop into that chair. Now your neighbour will see that your chair becomes empty, so they stand up, move to the left, and so on.'**

Practise the left wave move with the group. Stress that you have to wait until the left chair is empty before standing up.

> **'The "right wave" is the same as the left wave, but in the opposite direction.'**

Now practise both left and right waves. Start with the left wave, but then call 'right wave' so that the wave moves in the opposite direction. Change the direction of the wave a few times.

When the participants are familiar with the 2 waves, add the following rule:

> **'Now the person in the middle tries to sit down on the empty chair. They can only do this when the person who has to move is not quick enough. Then the new person, who was too late, stands in the middle and directs the wave.'**

When the group is skilled in both waves, add the 'hop waves'.

> **'Now we'll introduce "hop waves": in a left hop wave the person who moves is the person who sits second left from the empty chair. The person who sits first left of the empty chair sees this person "flying" over their lap.'**

Practise the left hop wave, and when participants understand this move introduce the right hop wave. Then mix all the waves together, as directed by the person in the middle.

Comment

This game creates a chaotic excitement and catches the attention of all participants. As in the other games where people change places, you can divide the circle in parts to form subgroups for the next activity. You may wish to add a debriefing.

Debriefing

- How was it to play this game?
- What did you enjoy?
- How was it to stand in the middle?

ROTTEN FRUIT
Change places with other fruits

Risk level: medium
Energy level: high
Number of participants: 12–50
Age: 6+

Time: 5 minutes
Materials: chairs, 1 for each participant

Explanation

Participants sit in a circle of chairs with one person in the middle – he or she is the 'rotten fruit'.

> **'Everyone in a chair thinks of a fruit and keeps it in mind.**
>
> **The person in the middle walks round within the circle and calls out the names of different fruits. If you hear your fruit called out, you get up and walk behind the rotten fruit.**
>
> **When there are several people behind the rotten fruit, then that person calls out "Fruit salad!" at which point everyone tries to grab a chair. The last person left standing becomes the rotten fruit and begins the process again.'**

Comment

If you use different subjects, try to have an appropriate phrase and name to replace 'rotten fruit' for the person in the middle. For example, for feelings you might call the person in the middle the 'therapist' and they call out 'psychotherapy!'

VARIATION

By changing the subject of this game can you can facilitate an exploration of different subjects. For example, the theme could be:

- feelings
- needs
- holiday ideas
- school subjects
- important skills in friendship
- things you are scared of.

4

FUN!

People love to laugh and play. In this chapter you will find a variety of energizers and games that have a sole purpose: fun!

When you announce the games, avoid telling the group the purpose. It is best just to introduce them as an experiment, an interlude or an exercise to stimulate the mind and body.

Use these games sparingly, to bring new energy into groups or at the start of a new lesson. To add to the fun, you can join in the games.

We haven't included a debriefing paragraph for most of the games in this chapter. However, many of the games may be readily adapted to explore specific issues with your groups. Develop your questions around the issues you would like to explore.

THE HAT OF AUNT MARIETTE
A call and response rhythm game

Energy level: medium
Number of participants: 12–50
Age: 8+

Time: 10 minutes
Materials: chairs for all
participants

Explanation

Participants sit in a circle in chairs. Give every chair a number from 1 up to the total number of chairs, and you sit in chair 1.

> **'We're going to play the game called the hat of Aunt Mariette. For this we have to clap a rhythm.'**

Clap your hands together, then clap your thighs with your hands in a slow, even rhythm: 1 – 2 – 1 – 2. The participants follow the rhythm.

> **'The person on chair number one always starts the game. They think of someone in the group, say Masha, and in rhythm chant: "Who has the hat of Aunt Mariette? Masha has the hat of Aunt Mariette."**
>> **Then Masha has to reply in the rhythm: "Who, me?"**
>> **And looking at Masha, the whole group replies: "Yes, you!"**
>> **Masha replies: "Not me!"**
>> **The group responds: "Then who?"**

Masha chooses someone else in the group and replies: "Frank has the hat of Aunt Mariette!"
And then Frank continues...'

To help the participants follow the words, write them on a flipchart:

The hat of Aunt Mariette

Leader starts with:
Who has the hat of Aunt Mariette?
Sammy has the hat of Aunt Mariette!

Sammy: Who, me?
All: Yes, you!
Sammy: Not me!
All: Then who?
Sammy: Lucy has the hat of Aunt Mariette!
Lucy: Who, me?
All: Yes, you!
Lucy: ...

Practise the game with a slow rhythm.

When all participants know the game, add the following rule:

'**If you get the rhythm or the words wrong you have to leave your chair and move to the last chair, and everyone who was after you moves up one place.**'

Continue to play. Every time someone makes a mistake, the people on their left move up a place. Allow yourself to make a mistake so that you too have to start at the end and the group has a new leader.

Comment

Once the participants know the game you can speed up the rhythm.

Though this game is listed in the fun section, as with most games it can be used as an introduction to important themes such as 'How one might react when someone says something to you', 'How to express yourself whilst clearly owning your experience' (in Gestalt, what is called an 'I-message') or 'How to defend yourself verbally'.

VARIATION: 'RHYTHM'

This variant is much the same as 'The hat of Aunt Mariette' except that instead of names chair numbers are used and the participants clap a special rhythm sentence.

Chalk a number in front of each chair. The person who starts the game sits on chair number 1.

Explain and demonstrate the rhythm sentence with movements:

What is said	Movement
rhythm...	Clap with both hands on lap.
ready...	Clap your hands.
5 (your own number)...	Click the fingers of your right hand.
7 (someone else's number)	Click the fingers of your left hand.

'The person on chair 1 starts the game with: "Rhythm ready 1," which is their own number, and then the number of someone in the circle, for example, "5". So, "Rhythm ready 1, 5."

Person number 5 responds, chanting: "Rhythm ready 5," and another number.

Every time your number is called, you take over and chant the rhythm sentence.

When you don't react quickly enough, or when you make a mistake, you have to sit on the last chair and everyone after you moves up one place. The aim is to become number 1.'

Experienced players can send the rhythm towards themselves by chanting their own number twice. Doing this they can speed up the rhythm and try to trick out the person on chair number 1.

COMMENT

Teenagers like this game. The added confusion of changing numbers when you change chairs increases the complexity, concentration and fun.

NAPOLEON HAS LOST HIS PIPE

A call and response word game

Energy level: medium
Number of participants: 12–50
Age: 8+

Time: 10 minutes
Materials: chairs for all
participants

Explanation

The aim of the game is to pass on the blame to someone else in the group, following a set form of words.

Participants sit or stand in a circle of chairs, with chairs numbered from 1 upwards.

> 'The person on chair 1 starts with: "Napoleon has lost his pipe, but Sir 'James' will bring it back."
>
> James responds with: "Tis not true, sir."
>
> The first person replies: "Then who, sir?"
>
> James responds: "Miss Kate, sir," passing the blame on to Kate.
>
> Kate responds to James: "Tis not true, sir!"
>
> James responds to Kate: "Then who, miss?"
>
> This continues until someone makes a mistake. If you make a mistake, such as getting the words or a name wrong, you move to the last chair and everyone to their left moves up one place.'

Practise the game a few times, ensuring that people use the correct form of words, addressing each other as 'sir' or 'miss', then play for real. Encourage expression and gesture to enhance the fun.

VARIATION

This is the same game but uses different words which are more difficult to pronounce. It starts with the King on the first chair, who turns to the person on their left (number 1).

> *The King starts:* '**Who killed King John?**'
>
> *Number 1 responds:* '**Not I.**'

King: **'Then who killed King John?'**

(Number 1 picks another number from the group – for example, 7.)

Number 1: **'Number 7 killed King John.'**

Number 7 responds: **'Not I.'**

Number 1: **'Then…'**

And so on, as above, with the person who makes an error moving to the end of the line.

GROUP JUGGLE
Juggling lots of balls with the group

Energy level: high

Number of participants: 12–30

Age: 8+

Time: 10 minutes

Materials: 12 soft balls

Explanation

Participants stand in a circle. Only show one ball, and give the following instruction:

> **'In the first round everyone is going to get this ball before it comes back to me.**
>
> **When you have the ball, call the name of someone who doesn't have their hand raised, throw the ball to them underarm and then raise your hand.**
>
> **Make sure you remember who you threw the ball to.'**

Demonstrate this. The ball is thrown from one participant to another and then returns to you.

> **'Now in the second round I will throw the ball to the same person as before, and then they will also throw to the person the same as before. This way the ball will follow the same route. Because this is a second round you only need to call the person's name,**

you don't need to raise your hand, and I will add an additional complexity. Everyone clear? Ready?'

Throw the ball to the same person you threw it to before, but then throw another ball to the same person, and another, and another, until all 12 are going round.

Enjoy the chaos and collect the balls when the last person throws them back to you.

Comment

Though you may give the instruction clearly, participants often still manage to miss something. Most of the time people enjoy the chaos but if it goes completely wrong start again, checking that everyone has understood.

VARIATION 1

Use 2 colours of balls. One colour goes in one direction, the other goes in the opposite one.

VARIATION 2

Throw imaginary balls, saying the colour. The participants can throw these 'balls' to anyone but continue to say the name of the person they throw to, and the colour of the ball.

VARIATION 3

Throw any imaginary object, saying what it is as you throw it. The catcher transforms the object into something else. For example: you start by throwing a pillow to Ann, Ann clutches the pillow and throws a bucket to John, John catches the bucket and throws a deckchair to Jane, and so on…

FRUPPLE

Passing a mysteriously named object around the group

Energy level: medium
Number of participants: 12–30
Age: 8+
Time: 10 minutes

Materials: any 2 objects to
represent the 'frupple' and the
'boing boing'

Explanation

Participants sit or stand in a circle.

> 'I have 2 special objects. When you pass it on to your neighbour
> you always say what it is: "This is a…" When you receive the
> object you always ask your neighbour what the object is by
> saying "A what?" They in turn ask the person who gave it to them
> saying, "A what?" and so on, back to me, and then I reply.
>
> When I have replied, the person with the object then passes it
> on, saying "This is a…"'

Start by passing one object to your right:

You: 'This is a frupple.'

Your neighbour: 'A what?'

You: 'A frupple.'

Your neighbour (number 1) gives this to the next neighbour (number 2): **'This is a frupple.'**

Neighbour 2 asks first neighbour 1: **'A what?'**

Neighbour 1 asks you: **'A what?'**

You say to neighbour 1: **'A frupple.'**

Neighbour 1 says to neighbour 2: **'A frupple.'**

Neighbour 2 says to neighbour 3: **'This is a frupple.'**

Neighbour 3 to neighbour 2: **'A what?'**

And so on.

When everyone has grasped the game, you introduce another object, following the same ritual and starting by passing it to your left:

You: **'This is a boing boing.'**

Left neighbour: **'A what?'**

You: **'A boing boing.'**

Left neighbour 1 to left neighbour 2: **'This is a boing boing.'**

And so on.

Comment

A fun game. Encourage the players to follow the correct ritual, though making mistakes is okay and contributes to the fun. When the objects cross it is confusing. Help the participants to follow the ritual until the objects return to you.

VARIATION

Same game, but this time with gestures.

A to B: **'I saw an elephant.'**

B to A: **'A what?'**

A to B: **'An elephant.'** (Show with gestures the big ears of the elephant.)

B to C: **'A** (e.g. Sally) **saw an elephant.'**

C to B: **'A what?'**

B to A: **'A what?'**

A to B: **'An elephant.'** (Show the ears.)

And so on.

'Going in the other direction, you start:'

A to Z: **'I saw a mouse.'**

Z to Y: **'A what?'**

A to Z: **'A mouse.'** (Imitate a mouse nibbling cheese.)

And so on.

THE SAMURAI
A fun Japanese strategy game

Energy level: high
Number of participants: 12–40
Age: 8+

Time: 10 minutes
Materials: masking tape or lines
marked on the floor

Explanation

Prepare the room by sticking masking tape in 2 parallel lines on the floor, approximately 150cm apart. The space between the lines is no-man's land.

Divide the group into 2 equal sides. The rival teams stand to either side of the lines.

'We are going to play an ancient Japanese war game.

There are 2 tribes trying to defeat each other. The tribes stand opposite each other outside of no-man's land.

Each time they meet the opposite tribe in battle, they have to choose one of 3 symbolic gestures. These are the samurai, the tiger, and the wise old woman. Each one of the characters has a gesture and a sound.

The samurai's gesture is like this.'

Show how the samurai, with sword raised, vertically stamps one foot forward as he yells **'Kia!'** Get everyone to practise together: **'3, 2, 1'**, and everyone does the samurai gesture and cry. Practise a couple of times until everyone does it with true 'samurai energy'.

'The tiger's gesture is like this.'

Put one foot forward, extending your hands out like claws, and with a fierce look in your eyes, roar **'Grahaa!'**

Practise the tiger gesture a few times together.

'The wise old woman's gesture is like this.'

Put your left hand on your hip, bend forward a little, right arm bent forward with your index finger raised, and with a toothless face chuckle: **'Heheheee!'**

Practise the wise old woman a few times.

'If a tribe does the samurai and the other tribe does the tiger then the tribe with samurai wins and gets one point because the samurai always beats the tiger.

But the tiger always beats the wise old woman, and the wise old woman always beats the samurai.

If both tribes make the same symbol, no one wins.

Before the tribes meet in their symbolic battle they discuss in secret which gesture they are all going to do.'

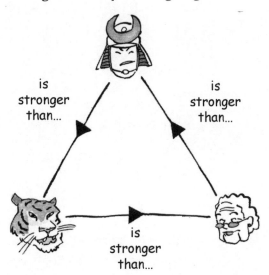

Both tribes go away and huddle to discuss which gesture they will use. They have a maximum of 30 seconds and then return to the line facing their opponents. When everyone is ready they say together **'Kon ni chi wa!'**, and on **'wa!'** both tribes make their gesture.

Give a point for the winning group. If it is a draw they make a very
formal ceremonial bow with palms touching, and say **'Ho'**. Keep the
score and play for 5 minutes or so.

Comment

This is a high energy and volume game.

You can use this game to introduce a workshop about collective decision-
making and taking initiative.

HILARIOUS VARIATION

Make a base camp for each tribe so that they can hide from each other.

Use the same rules as above, but when the tribes show their gesture the
tribe who loses has to flee to their den.

At the same time the winning tribe members chase, and try to tag, the
fleeing tribe. If you are tagged you join the new tribe and help them to try
to win the game. It is possible to change sides several times.

Play until the time is up or everyone has become a member of the same
tribe.

THE STORM

Cool down, listening to the sound of the rain

Energy level: medium–high
Number of participants: 12–40
Age: 8+

Time: 10 minutes
Materials: none

Explanation

Participants sit in a circle.

> **'I want you to copy the movements and gestures of the person on your right. If they stop, or change their movement, you follow their lead. As well as watching I'd particularly like you to keep your ears open.'**

Start rubbing your palms together. Gradually the whole group joins in, as they copy their neighbour. When everyone is following begin to blow, making a sound like the wind. Again, when everyone is following, begin the next sound:

- click your fingers (until everyone does this)
- clap your hands on your lap
- clap your hands on your lap and stamp your feet
- clap your hands on your lap

- click your fingers
- rub your palms
- put your hands on your lap.

If it works out well you will hear the wind, the rain, storm, thunder, and then end with a peaceful silence.

Comment

This activity is helpful to bring some quiet and rest to a group. If the participants like the game, encourage them to create new variations in which they can lead the group. Or suggest themes that they can compose around, such as the beach, a train journey...

VARIATION

A more hilarious version involves asking participants to imitate sounds of the jungle. The following sequence of sounds can be used:

- hiss of a snake
- chirping of a cricket
- cry of a monkey
- 'hello' of a parrot
- chest beating of a gorilla
- roar of a lion
- and in reverse, back to the hiss of the snake.

THE ZOO
Visual group reaction game

crocodile

fish

elephant

Energy level: high
Number of participants: 12–40
Age: 8+

Time: 10–20 minutes
Materials: none

Explanation

Participants stand in a closed circle and you stand in the middle as the first zookeeper.

> 'The aim is to avoid ending up as the zoo keeper.
>
> The zoo keeper calls someone's name and an animal that lives in the Zoo of Zazawie, which is a very poor zoo with only an elephant, a crocodile and a fish.
>
> As soon as you hear your name and the animal, you must quickly perform the gesture of the animal. The people either side of you must also make their appropriate gestures.
>
> If you or they are too slow, or if anyone gets the gesture even slightly wrong, then the zookeeper identifies who, and they become the new zoo keeper. Let's practise the animals before we start playing...'

Be specific about how the gestures are performed, and strict as the zoo keeper.

For the elephant pinch your nose with one hand and pass your other arm through the loop as the trunk. Your partners on either side make an ear from shoulder to hip. (See the picture.)

> **'For example, if I say "Natasha Elephant" then Natasha makes the trunk of the elephant and the people either side of her make the ears.'**

For the crocodile:

> **'If I say "Sylvia Crocodile" then Sylvia makes the head with 2 stretched arms and the neighbours make an eye on top of the head. These eyes come out of the water.'** (See picture.)

For the fish:

> **'If I say "Paul Fish" then Paul makes the mouth of the fish opening and closing his mouth like a goldfish and his neighbours make the fins by fluttering their hands by his waist.'** (See picture.)

Practise the 3 animals a few times with different people. Then begin by saying someone's name, and one of the animals, without looking at them.

When the rules of the game are clear, be strict. If people don't respond quickly enough, or get the gesture wrong, they become the zoo keeper.

Play the game for about 5 minutes.

Comment

This game enables people to move, laugh and play, and at the same time promotes concentration, so is good preparation for an activity which requires stillness and concentration.

VARIATION 1: IN THE KITCHEN

If the group wants to play the game again, then you can replace the types with objects from the kitchen:

'**Sabine Toaster: the neighbours form a square box with their arms around Sabine and Sabine jumps up and down.**

Kurt Mixer: Kurt stretches his arms left and right above the heads of the neighbours. The neighbours spin around vertically as if they are the whisks of the mixer.

Jessica Washing Machine: the neighbours form a circle around Jessica's hips and she turns around, gyrating her hips as if she was hula-hooping.'

VARIATION 2: SELF-DEFENCE

This variation can be used to introduce the theme of physical or emotional self-defence or 'taking care of yourself'.

The rules of the game are the same as to begin with, but instead of animals, you learn the following 3 positions:

'**Emilia Karate: Emilia does one big step forwards and cuts an invisible wooden board in 2 with a karate chop, yelling: "Kia!" Both neighbours take a karate stance and pull their elbows into their waists whilst making a fist, and say: "Huss!"**

Jim Boxing: Jim gets into boxer's position and throws a punch. The neighbours tap Jim on the shoulder and say: "Dish dish!"

Jeff Taekwando: Jeff does a kick straight ahead, makes a fist and yells: "Haa!" The neighbours place one foot forwards, push out with both hands and yell: "Chi!"

ESP
Mind-reading and telepathy

Energy level: high
Number of participants: 12–40
Age: 8+

Time: 10 minutes
Materials: none

Explanation

Make groups of 3.

> **'I want to check if some groups have ESP, extra-sensory perception. We are going to check this out by having 3 distinct postures.'**

Demonstrate the following postures and have the participants imitate you.

- *The kangaroo:* bend your knees as you would to sit on a chair, hold your arms in front of your chest and bend your wrists.

- *The ballerina:* stand on your toes, one leg crossing the other, and arms raised above your head with fingers overlapping.

- *The thinker:* kneel on your left knee, put your right elbow on your right knee, and rest your forehead on the closed fist of your right hand.

> **'Okay, nod if you know the 3 postures.'**

Look around to check that everyone is nodding.

'What I'd like you to do is close your eyes and concentrate on the 2 other people in your group... Connect with them on a deep, deep level of intuition. Recollect the 3 postures and on "1!" I'd like you all to adopt a posture and then open your eyes to see how your group did.

So think of the 3 positions... 3, 2, 1!'

Look around to see how the groups got on and celebrate the groups that all have the same pose. Repeat this activity several times to see which group really has ESP.

Comment

Of course this activity has nothing to do with ESP. You can use this game to introduce the theme of active listening, imagining, and guessing what someone feels and thinks.

Listening is a vital life skill.

You can also relate this game to expressing requests – often we don't express our needs and requests, hoping others will guess. It might be obvious to us what we want, but that is not the case for others. Learn to value your needs and to express them.

Debriefing

• How did you find this activity?

VARIATION

'In this game you need ESP to survive. Walk criss-cross around the room and choose a number – either 2, 4 or 6. Have a clear sense of this number in your mind and then tune in to who else has the same number.

When you are confident, approach them and shake hands 2, 4 or 6 times. If you have chosen someone with a different number, you will both notice that one wants to stop while the other wants to carry on, in which case you are both out.

If you have the same number you survive and participate in the next round. Once again choose a number and tune in to who has the same number, then approach them and see.'

Play this game several times until some real 'ESP-people' remain.

If there is an even number of participants you can observe, but if the number is uneven you can take part.

You can make this version more fun by adding a staged death if you choose the wrong partner.

PUDDING
Hilarious interlude

Energy level: high

Number of participants: 8–40

Age: 8+

Time: 10 minutes

Materials: none

Explanation

Participants sit in a circle and each person in turn names their favourite dessert/pudding. Each dessert/pudding can only be chosen once, so that everyone's is different.

When you have been round the circle and each person has spoken, explain the rules:

> **'Each player passes the pudding to another player, first naming their own favourite pudding and then the other player's pudding.'**
>
> *Chocolate mousse to start:* **'For example, chocolate mousse to vanilla cheesecake, vanilla cheesecake to lemon meringue pie, lemon meringue pie to strawberry ice cream, and so on.'**

Once the general form of the game is understood, introduce the most important rule, which is that no one is allowed to laugh. What determines whether you are laughing or not is if you show your teeth.

'So now you have to name your favourite pudding, and the pudding of the person you are passing to, while hiding your teeth with your lips.

If anyone makes a mistake in passing the game on, or laughs, then the other participants clasp their hands behind their head, point at the offending player with their elbows and exclaim: "Pudding! Pudding!" waggling their elbows but obviously not showing their teeth!'

Comment

Introduce the second part of the game by demonstrating not showing your teeth as you explain the rules. This way the participants can see what is expected of them.

This game may not be well received by serious people who are intent on avoiding looking silly, but we have found that sometimes by playing it serious people can let go and enjoy the crazy nature of the game.

EVOLUTIONARY GAME
An evolutionary version of 'Paper – scissors – stone'

Energy level: high
Number of participants: 12–40
Age: 8+

Time: 10 minutes
Materials: none

Explanation

Explain the game 'Paper – scissors – stone'.

Two players stand opposite each other with a closed fist, lifting and lowering their hand to a count of 3. On '3' they shape their hand as paper, scissors or stone.

- *Paper*: open, flat hand.
- *Scissors*: index and middle finger open, rest of the fingers closed.
- *Stone*: closed fist.

Paper wraps stone, stone blunts scissors and scissors cut paper. Practise this until everyone is clear on the rules of the game.

> **'Now in this game the aim is to evolve into a human being. We all start as an amoeba. To show that you are an amoeba you make swimming movements with your arms and say, "Amoeba, amoeba."'**

Demonstrate the movement and ask the participants to copy you.

'When 2 amoebas meet they play paper – scissors – stone and the winner becomes a frog. The frog hops around, has arms in front like a tyrannosaurus rex and croaks.'

Demonstrate the frog and ask the group to copy you.

'When 2 frogs meet they play paper – scissors – stone. The winning frog then becomes a gorilla. To show that you are a gorilla you swagger around with bow-legs, beat your chest and exclaim: "Whu whu whu!"'

Demonstrate the movement and ask the participants to copy you.

'When 2 gorillas meet they play paper – scissors – stone. The winner becomes a human. When you are a human take a seat and enjoy the spectacle.'

Comment

Excellent fun game.

The last remaining amoeba, frog and gorilla automatically become humans and take a seat.

POKER FACE

Keep your expression under control…

Energy level: high
Number of participants: 12–40
Age: 8+

Time: 10 minutes
Materials: none

Explanation

Ask the participants to line up in 2 rows facing each other, forming a 'tunnel' that someone can walk down.

Ask for one volunteer from each row, someone who is able to keep a straight face. They then stand at either end of the 'tunnel', facing each other.

> 'So the goal is to keep a "poker face" for longer than your opponent. You must hold each other's gaze as you walk slowly down the rows towards your opponent. The people in the row will try to make both players smile or laugh.
>
> When you meet in the middle you shake hands and greet each other in a rather formal and dry manner, saying, "Hello, how are you today?" You then pass each other and continue to the end of the row.
>
> If you can complete this task without laughing, your mission is accomplished.

The people in the rows will keep an eye on you to make sure you are not smiling or laughing, and if you are then they wag their finger at you and call out, in a strict, deep voice (if they are women) or a high-pitched voice (if they are men): "Poker face!"'

Give a signal to start and let the players begin their task. The one who maintains their poker face the longest wins. If both candidates succeed the group applauds them.

Give everyone who wants a go a chance to play.

Comment

This exercise is a helpful route into exploring the themes of self-control, dealing with group pressure and making choices regardless of what others want.

Debriefing

- Was it hard not to laugh? And if so, why do you think that was?
- Did you manage to concentrate, and if so, what helped?
- Or what went wrong?
- How did you find this game?

FORESTER
Recognize someone by the sound of their voice

Energy level: medium–high
Number of participants: 12–30
Age: 5+

Time: 10 minutes
Materials: 1 blindfold

Explanation

Participants stand or sit in a circle; you then blindfold a volunteer who becomes the forester, standing in the middle.

Now everyone in the circle changes places, and you give each person a number: 1, 2, 3, and so on.

'The forester in the middle must try to recognize the animals in the forest. The forester will call a number and that person will make the sound of an animal. The forester has to try to guess which person made that sound.'

If the forester guesses right, someone else becomes the forester.

VARIATION

Instead of making an animal sound the participants say a short phrase like: 'I'm hungry.' They can disguise their voices to avoid being recognized.

WINK MURDER
Find the winking killer

Energy level: medium–high
Number of participants: 12–30
Age: 5+

Time: 10 minutes
Materials: pack of cards

Explanation

Prepare a pack of cards, one card for each player, including a jack of spades and the 4 queens.

Everyone takes a random card.

> '**Check what your card is without letting anyone else see it. If you have the jack of spades you are the killer, and you kill people by winking at them. If someone winks at you wait a moment, or take 3 steps, before dying theatrically.**
>
> **The 4 queens are detectives whose aim is to catch the killer before he kills anyone. If one of the queens thinks she knows the murderer she points at the suspect and declares in a posh voice, "Sir (madam/miss), I arrest you in the name of the law," and the person then shows their card. If the guess is wrong then the queen is out.**
>
> **The aim for the killer is to kill everyone, including the queens, before he is caught.'**

Participants criss-cross the room during the game.

Repeat this a few times so that a number of people get to play the different roles.

Comment

Young people enjoy the opportunity of looking into each others' eyes in the safe context of this game. It can be a good introduction to exploring the theme of 'making contact with someone you like' and flirting.

MY BONNIE LIES OVER THE OCEAN

Sing and move

Energy level: high
Number of participants: 12–30
Age: 7+

Time: 10 minutes
Materials: none

Explanation

Everyone sits in a circle.

Sing the song 'My bonnie lies over the ocean'.[1]

'We are going to sing the song again, and whenever we sing a "b" we stand up, and with the next "b" we sit down, and so on.'

Sing the song together, and with every 'b' the group stands up or sits down. Sing the song again with variants, such as:

- With every 'b' one participant stands up. When everyone is standing, participants sit down one by one with each successive 'b'.

- Half the group start standing and the other half sitting. When the sitters sing a 'b' they stand up, and those standing sit down, and so on through the song.

---

1   Find the lyrics and melody on the internet if you don't know it.

- Split the group in 2. The first group reacts on the first 'b', the second group on the second 'b', the first group reacts again on the next 'b', and so on.

Comment

Singing often generates a relaxed atmosphere that may lead to another song.

PEEP CANARY

Sing together with inner voice

Energy level: medium–high
Number of participants: 12–30
Age: 7+

Time: 10 minutes
Materials: none

Explanation

Learn the following song. If you can't read the music, then create a melody to fit the words:

peep ca   nary   peep ca nary peep ca nary peep ca nary

peep ca nary peep ca nary peep ca nary PEEP!

When everyone knows the song we then add some variation, keeping the same tune and timing but missing out some of the words.

1. 'We sing the song but the word "canary" is silent, so we only hear "peep".'

2. 'We sing only the first and last "peep".'

3. 'We sing the song but the word "peep" is silent and "canary" is aloud.'

4. 'We sing the song twice but sing only the first and the last "peep".'

5. 'We sing the song once with our eyes closed, singing only the first and last "peep".'

Comment

Singing with the inner voice creates a bond. You will notice that participants look in each others' eyes to follow the rhythm. Insist that they sing in time and encourage listening and concentration so that they improve.

1, 2, 3, LOOK
Making eye contact

Energy level: medium–high
Number of participants: 12–30
Age: 5+

Time: 10 minutes
Materials: none

Explanation

The participants stand in a circle.

'First all look at the ground. I will say: "1, 2, 3, look." When I say "look" then you immediately look at someone. If that person is also looking at you, then you are both out and leave the circle.'

Call '1, 2, 3, look', and participants who are looking at each other leave the circle. Repeat the activity until only one or 2 people are left. Celebrate the winners.

You can play the game again if the participants enjoy it.

Comment

Young people like to experiment with eye contact and this game provides a safe context in which to explore that.

It is also a good game for new groups where people are still checking each other out.

This game can be used as an introduction to exploring themes of looking at and being looked at, subject and object, and making contact with people. There is also the element of projection, as with 'Who might look at me? Who can I rely on?'

Debriefing

- How did you find this game?
- How did you find making eye contact with people?
- How was it to be looked at?

VARIATION 1

When 2 players find that they are looking at each other, then instead of having to leave the circle permanently they just have to run around the circle once and return to their positions.

You can make it more fun by introducing things that those running around have to do – for example, making duck noises as they run.

VARIATION 2

With smaller groups you can change the game. Instead of being 'out' if you *do* make eye contact, this time you lose a life if you *don't* have eye contact. You can't look at the same person consecutively, and you have 3 lives before you are 'out'.

SIMPLE SIMON DIED

A crazy game that gets crazier as it goes on

Hawwwe yooou heaaard oowhaot...

Energy level: medium–high
Number of participants: 6–15
Age: 5+

Time: 10 minutes
Materials: flipchart with the script from the box below

Simple Simon

A: Have you heard what happened to Simple Simon?

B: No, what happened?

A: Simple Simon met his end.

B: And how did he meet his end?

A: With 2 fingers in his mouth.

Explanation

Participants stand or sit in a circle.

'We are going to speak about Simple Simon and it goes as follows.'

You begin performing the dialogue on the flipchart with the person on your left. You play role A and they play B. When you say the last sentence you put 2 spread fingers in your mouth.

'The person on your left then passes on the news of Simple Simon to the person on their left. Whilst doing this they have 2 fingers spread in their mouth, and after the last sentence they add another detail of how Simple Simon died – for example, with shaking knees.

   The next person starts the same dialogue with their left neighbour, with 2 fingers in their mouth, and shaking knees, and they add another element in the last sentence.'

Each player adds a new detail as it proceeds around the circle, until it is impossible to do or a player can't perform the dialogue because they are laughing so much. Then start again from the beginning.

Comment

A fun game to bring some light energy to a group after a heavy discussion.

THE MOLE CATCHER
Avoid being caught by the mole catcher

Energy level: medium–high
Number of participants: 12–30
Age: 5+

Time: 15 minutes
Materials: 40 metres of rope,
blindfold for each participant

Explanation

With the help of 4 people, one at each corner, use the rope to prepare an area approximately 10 by 10 metres. The rope needs to be held tightly, about a metre high, to keep the participants safe.

Everyone has a blindfold, except a volunteer who is the mole catcher. The moles stand in the ring with their blindfolds off.

'In the ring you are blind moles and the mole catcher is going to try to catch all of you. The moles are quiet and can move faster than the mole catcher, while the mole catcher growls and stamps with every step he takes.'

Now the moles all stand in the middle of the ring and put their blindfolds on. Then the mole catcher enters the ring with one loud stamp and a growl.

Because the moles are in the middle, the mole catcher cannot touch them yet.

Each time tell the moles how many steps they can take, followed by the instruction for the mole catcher. Always allow the moles more steps than the mole catcher. For example:

The moles can take 3 steps. So tell the mole catcher:

'Two steps, mole catcher!'

The mole catcher growls and stamps 2 steps, trying to touch as many moles as possible. Moles that are touched are out. They remove their blindfold, and leave the arena.

VARIATION

Allow the mole catcher to decide how many steps to take and the moles are always allowed twice that number of steps.

GIANT CLOCKS

Show the time with your body

Energy level: medium
Number of participants: 12–50
Age: 10+

Time: 5 minutes
Materials: none

Explanation

Participants stand in a circle or stand randomly in the space.

> **'We all change into big clocks. Pretend that your left arm is the long hand and your right arm is the short hand.'**

Call out a time and the participants show the time with their arms.

> **'Show me 12 o'clock.**
> **Show 6 o'clock.**
> **Show 9 o'clock.**
> **Half past 2.'**

Now each participant in turn calls out a time, and the others show the time with their arms.

Comment

A simple game to boost the energy of a group that needs movement and air.

THE GIANT'S TREASURE
Steal the treasure, avoiding the blind giant

Energy level: medium–high
Number of participants: 12–40
Age: 4+
Time: 10 minutes

Materials: tin box with marbles/
beans/coins, blindfold,
newspaper

Explanation

Draw a circle of 5 metres' diameter and place the treasure (a noisy tin box)
in the middle of the circle. The participants sit around the edge of the
circle.

One person, who becomes the giant, is blindfolded and has a roll of
newspaper or a boffer as their club. The giant's task is to stop the rascals
stealing the box.

> **'The goal for those on the edge is to steal and escape with the**
> **treasure from the centre. If the giant catches you with his club**
> **you are out. If you get clubbed whilst escaping with the treasure,**
> **you have to put it down where you are and leave.'**

Give each person in turn a chance to steal the treasure.

If the rascals succeed, then start again with a new giant.

Comment

Organize the game so that only one person at a time attempts to steal the treasure.

VARIATION

You can play with 2 giants and/or 2 rascals at the same time.

TAP, TAP

Reaction game tapping on each others' knees

Energy level: high
Number of participants: 12–40
Age: 4+

Time: 10 minutes
Materials: none

Explanation

Participants sit in a circle.

> **'Put your right hand on the left knee of your right neighbour and put your left hand on the right knee of your left neighbour.'**

Demonstrate what you want to help the group understand.

> **'Now we are going to tap our hands clockwise.'** (Indicate the direction for younger children.)

The participants tap their left hands on the knee of their left neighbour, who in turn passes the tap around the circle in a clockwise direction.

> Practise also the anti-clockwise direction.

> **'Now we add another rule: when someone taps twice, the direction of the tapping changes.'**

Practise this rule. Every time someone makes a mistake by not following the order, start again.

'Now we add another rule: when someone makes a mistake by tapping too early, too late or in the wrong direction, the culprit puts their hand behind their back. The order of play still has to be followed, even though some of the hands are missing.'

Play the game until everyone is out (i.e. has both hands behind their backs) or you run out of time.

Comment

Be strict in the judgement of a mistake: for example, when someone lifts their hand but doesn't tap this could already be a mistake if out of order.

When you play the game for a second or third time, play it at a faster pace.

LAUGHING CIRCLE
A mock serious laughing exercise

Energy level: high
Number of participants: 12–40
Age: 4+

Time: 10 minutes
Materials: none

Explanation

Participants stand in a circle.

Introduce the exercise in a mock serious way (see the example below). Feel free to embellish the positive health benefits of laughter, and also use language appropriate to the age group you are working with.

> **'Research has shown that laughing is good for your health. It promotes the absorption of oxygen. The sound and movement of the diaphragm stimulates the auto-immune system and establishes a positive vibration in the heart. In the Far East, laughing is a part of general health education. I will show you a few laughs and invite you to imitate them.'**

Demonstrate the following laughs, which the group repeats:

- Haaaaaaaaaaa haaaa haaaaaa (royal laugh).
- Hohohohohohohohohohohoho (steamer laugh).
- Hihihihihihihi (fast dwarf's laugh).

- Huhuhuhuhuhu (toothless laugh).

- Heuheuheuheuheu (Scandinavian laugh).

- Wuu-a-a-a-wu-a-a-a (gorilla laugh).

- Make a smile.

- Hehahahaheera hahaha (high hysterical laugh).

- Psst psrstst prrrpsst (suppressed hysteric laugh).

- Woohahahahahaaa wuuuuuhahahaha (roaring laugh).

- Herherherherherrr (menacing laugh).

- Ha ha ha ha (James Bond baddie laugh).

Feel free to invent more laughs.

> 'We are going to pass laughs around the circle. When your neighbour demonstrates a laugh, turn around and perform the same laugh to the next person, who in turn passes it on around the circle.'

Make a royal laugh to your left neighbour, then a high hysterical laugh to your right neighbour. On both sides the participants pass the laughs on. A tricky moment comes when the 2 laughs have to cross each other.

Comment

This laughing game often ends in uncontrolled group laughter.

LAUGHING ON A BIKE
Laughing exercise for bikers

Energy level: high
Number of participants: 12–40
Age: 12+

Time: 10 minutes
Materials: none (except an imaginary motorbike)

Explanation

Participants stand in a circle.

Explain that laughing is good for people's health because it provides the body with oxygen. (See previous game, 'Laughing circle'.) Invite the participants to follow the exercise:

> **'Today we are going to take a ride on our laughing Harley-Davidson motorbike. Imagine that before you there is this beautiful machine – something you have dreamed of for many years. Take a deep breath and laugh out your joy: "Hahahahahaha…"'**

Laugh out loud to facilitate warm and playful engagement with the exercise for all the participants.

> **'So let's sit on the bike. Smile and enjoy. This bike is old-fashioned so you have to kick start it.'**

Show how to kickstart the bike, but with each attempt there is a dry 'hahahahaha'. Do this 3 times before announcing there must be a problem.

'Ooow...no petrol! Okay, we'll have to put some laughing gas in the tank. Screw off the petrol cap. Pour the laughing gas in... Hahahahahahahahahaa...

Screw the cap back on the tank. Dispose of the petrol can. Let's try again. Hopefully it'll work now.'

Kick start the bike: 'Hahahahahaha'. After a third attempt the motor turns: 'Hahahahahahaha...'

'Now the motor is running make a few laughing tours around the room and greet your fellow bikers with a laugh and a wave. But keep your eyes on the road.'

The participants ride their laughing bikes around the room, greeting the other road users.

Comment

This energizer is a pleasant interlude for a group that likes to laugh. Announce the activity as an experiment. As with most games it is important that you as the initiator enjoy doing the activity yourself.

SAUSAGE
Say 'sausage' without laughing

Energy level: medium
Number of participants: 12–40
Age: 6+

Time: 10 minutes
Materials: none

Explanation

Ask for a volunteer for a difficult activity, one that requires concentration and self-control.

Ask the person to sit on a chair facing you, but clearly visible to the rest of the group.

> **'I am going to ask you some questions to which you must always answer "sausage". If you laugh or answer anything other than "sausage" you are out.**
>
> **First question: are you ready? The correct answer to this question is "sausage".'**

You may choose to give the first person a chance if they get this question wrong.

> **'Okay, concentrate…'**

Ask the participant a number of questions, for example:

- What is your name?

- What is my name?
- What is the name of the head teacher?
- Do you have any pets?
- Where do you live?
- What is your mother's name?
- 2 plus 2 equals?
- Do you have any brothers and sisters?
- What are their names?
- What are you wearing on your feet?
- What do you have in your pocket?
- What is your best friend's name?
- How do you come to school?
- What would you like to be when you grow up?
- What is your nose like?

Allow a minute or 2 or until they smile or laugh, and celebrate anyone who manages to succeed.

Then ask for another volunteer, and so on.

Debriefing

- How did you find this game?
- What made you laugh?
- Why was it difficult to answer with the word 'sausage'?
- What helped you to keep a straight face?
- How might the ability of not reacting be helpful?

VARIATION

Form pairs and give the following assignment:

> **'Play the sausage game. The person with the darkest hair starts asking questions. Count how many times the other is able to respond with "sausage" without laughing, and when you are ready, change roles.'**

Usually participants have a lot of fun playing this game.

COMMENT

A suitable game to introduce themes such as responding to unpleasant stimuli, insults and provocation.

TARZAN
Brain gym in a jungle story

Energy level: high
Number of participants: 6–500
Age: 6+

Time: 10 minutes
Materials: none

Explanation

Ask the participants to imagine that they are Tarzan (or Jane, if they would prefer) and invite them to copy your movements and instructions, starting from where they are sitting.

> **'Tarzan (or Jane) is sleeping and lies lazily on the branch of a high tree in the jungle.'**

You slouch to one side of the chair to demonstrate.

> **'Tarzan hears the birds singing. He opens one eye, looks around. He doesn't see any birds but he does see some other slouchy Tarzans and Janes in other trees.**
>
> **He closes his eye and opens the other eye, then he closes that eye and opens both eyes. He looks to his left, looks to the right, he looks up, he looks down and then rolls his eyes one way and the other.**
>
> **Tarzan then pulls in his knees and sits upright. He stretches his left arm, his right arm, his left leg, his right leg.**

Tarzan still feels sleepy in his face. He starts massaging his eyes very gently, his cheeks, his nose, his upper lip, his mouth, chin, throat, neck, the back of his head then all of his skull.

The ears are very important so he gives them lots of love and attention... So many energy points that are connected with the whole body. First he rubs his hands to warm them up. Then he starts massaging the top of the ears, slowly moving to the lower parts, moving down and gently squeezing every little spot of the ear and finally massaging the ear lobes. Mmm...feels like he is becoming more awake.

Tarzan starts tapping his chest, breathing in and breathing out and making a deep sound with his voice: "OOOOOOOooooo..."

Tarzan is already pretty awake. To let the animals of the jungle know that he is awake he bends a little bit at his knees, breaths in, puts his hands left and right beside his mouth and shouts: "WUUUAAAAOOOOeeeiii..."

To calm his excitement Tarzan sits down again, takes a deep breath and sings "OOOOOOOOOOOOOOmmmmmmmmm". He repeats this, breathing OM 2 times, and Tarzan is ready for a new day.'

VARIATION

You can enrich the story by adding some of the following:

'Tarzan prepares for the meeting with the cross monkeys. So he practises the "cross monkey walk".' (Demonstrate touching the left knee with the right hand and the right knee with the left hand. Develop it further by touching the knee with the opposite elbow. Move on to touching the left heel with the right hand again, followed by the opposite diagonal.)

'Let us also prepare for the ritual greeting of the chief monkey.' (Slap both hands on your thighs, slap your chest, squeeze your nose with your left hand and squeeze your left ear with your right hand. Repeat: slap both hands on your thighs, slap your chest, squeeze your nose with your right hand and squeeze your right ear with your left hand.)

'Tarzan prepares for the meeting with the elephants, and practises the elephant greeting.' (Cross your arms at the elbows, squeeze your nose with the hand of the lower arm and weave an infinity sign with the trunk-arm.)

COMMENT

Nice game to start a day when participants ask for a special energizer. The exercises in the story are related to brain-gym activities, which activate parts of the brain and connections between different parts of the body.

FALLING LEAF

Concentrate, and react when you hear your name

Energy level: high
Number of participants: 12–50
Age: 6+

Time: 5 minutes
Materials: sheet of paper (variants: old plate, broom), chairs

Explanation

Participants sit in a circle on chairs. Stand in the middle of the circle with a sheet of paper on the tips of your fingers as high as possible.

'I am going to drop this paper…'

Drop it and with the participants watch how it falls. Then you retrieve it.

'This time when I drop it I will call a name. The objective is to try to catch it before it lands. If you catch the paper you tear the sheet in half, so the paper you hold is half the size. Now you stand in the middle, holding the smaller piece of paper high on the tips of your fingers, and call someone's name as you let the paper fall. They have to catch it before it lands.

If you cannot catch the paper, then you go into the middle without tearing it in half, hold it on the tips of your fingers, call someone's name and let it fall.'

Call the name of a participant and that person tries to catch the paper. With each success the paper size halves, and then the next person must catch it to succeed.

Play until just a small shred remains.

Comment

Use paper with the weight of notepaper or lighter. If you drop the sheet you can show how to make it more aerodynamic by curling the sides a little, so that it will glide elegantly.

VARIATION 1

This is the same exercise as above but instead of dropping a sheet of paper, you spin a plate. The person whose name is called has to catch the plate before it stops, and they then give the plate another spin, calling out someone else's name.

Use old plates on a soft, flat surface.

VARIATION 2

This is the same exercise as above but instead of dropping a sheet of paper or spinning a plate, you balance a broom. The person whose name is called has to catch the broom before it falls to the ground.

Make the exercise more demanding by having the participants lie on their tummy in the circle.

HORSE RACE

Body contact and fun in the horse race

Energy level: high
Number of participants: 12–50
Age: 6+

Time: 5 minutes
Materials: none

Explanation

Participants kneel in a very tight circle.

> **'I want to invite you to join me in the horse race. I will tell you what happens and show you what to do.'**

Describe the horse race (left column below) and demonstrate what happens (right column below). The participants mimic what you do.

'The horses walk to the starting line.'	Slap with the hands on your thighs.
'The horses concentrate for the start.'	Place both hands with outstretched arms in front of your knees. Make some nervous horse noises.
'Start! The horses start in a trot.'	Slap a trot-rhythm on your thighs.

'We are going round a right bend.'	Lean into your right neighbour and keep on slapping the trot-rhythm.
'We are back on the straight.'	Sit upright again and trot further.
'And round a left bend.'	Lean into your left neighbour and trot further.
'We want to win, so we go into a gallop.'	Make a gallop-rhythm, slapping on your thighs.
'A bend to the left.'	Lean into your left neighbour and keep on slapping the gallop-rhythm.
'Go straight.'	Sit upright again and gallop further.
'A bend to the right.'	Lean into your right neighbour and keep on slapping the gallop-rhythm.
'We have to jump over the creek.'	Sit upright and mime a jump with your hands a half metre in front of your knees.
'The finish line is in sight, full power!'	Slap a heavy gallop-rhythm on the thighs. Lift your butt off your heels.
'The horses cross the finish line and greet their owners.'	Slow down the rhythm to a trot, and blow between your lips.

Comment

Teenagers like this game because of the crazy humour and the fact that they can make body contact.

VARIATION

The following figures can be added according to your taste and the group's enthusiasm.

'The horses prepare for a picture in the newspaper.'	Make a BIG smile by pulling the corners of your mouth with your little fingers and showing your teeth.
'The riders greet the spectators on the terraces.'	Sit upright and wave.
'The rider greets a friend.'	Lift your right index finger and wink.
'The mobile of the rider rings.'	Search for a mobile and answer it.

RACING BALLS

Two teams compete to have the fastest ball

Energy level: high
Number of participants: 12–50
Age: 6+

Time: 5 minutes
Materials: 2 balls of the same size and different colours

Explanation

Participants stand in a circle. Number off 1s and 2s around the circle. Give one ball to a number 1 and one ball to a number 2, on opposite sides of the circle.

> **'We have a practice round before we start: the number 1s pass their ball around to the left from number 1s to number 1s, skipping number 2s in between. Number 2s do the same, passing their ball around to members of the 2 group.'**

Both groups pass their ball from one member to the next one. Stop the balls and explain the rest of the game.

> **'Now we are going to have a race between the 2 teams. The goal is to pass your ball around the whole of your group faster than the other team, with the aim of catching their ball. You can't impede or disturb the other team when the ball comes past you.'**

Start the game. Usually it takes some time before one ball catches the other, unless someone drops their ball.

Play a round or 3, and the winning team wins a round of applause.

VARIATIONS

- Let the participants pass a big pillow or a bandanna instead of a ball.
- Have the players pass the ball behind their backs.
- Have the participants stand in a line. Play the same game as above, but when the ball arrives at the end the last person runs to the beginning and gives the ball to the first one in their team.

BALLOON GAME
Juggling balloons with the group

Energy level: high
Number of participants: 4–30
Age: 6+

Time: 10 minutes
Materials: 5 balloons

Explanation

Participants stand in a circle. Number them off so that everyone has a number from 1 upwards.

Show them the balloon.

'One by one we are going to pat the balloon to keep it in the air, but we have to do it in numerical order.'

One by one the participants touch the balloon. Everyone calls out their number.

Now introduce a second balloon.

'Now we do the same with 2 balloons, continuing in numerical order as before for both.'

When one of the balloons falls, start again.

VARIATIONS

- Touch the balloon with the head only.
- Touch the balloon with the feet only.
- Touch the balloon with anything but the hands.

ARGH NI GO
Funny, Far Eastern reaction game

Energy level: high

Number of participants: 12–30

Age: 8+

Time: 15 minutes

Materials: none

Explanation

Participants stand in a circle.

> **'This is an exotic Far Eastern reaction game. In this game there are 3 gestures.**
>
> > **The first gesture is "Argh".'**

Show the 'Argh' gesture: bring your hand quickly up to shoulder height, as if you are about to do a karate chop on a block. (You can choose either your left or your right arm.) Exclaim: **'Argh!'** Practise the 'Argh' gesture with the participants.

> **'The person standing next to the hand raised in the "Argh" gesture demonstrates the "Ni" gesture.'**

Show the 'Ni' gesture: raise your left or right hand above your head, with the fingers of the stretched hand pointing left or right. Say loudly: **'Ni!'** Practise the 'Ni' with the participants.

'The person who is pointed at with the "Ni" gesture makes the "Go" gesture.'

Show the 'Go' gesture: point your fist at someone and exclaim: **'Go!'** and say the name of the person you are pointing at. Practise the 'Go' with the participants.

Practise the rules slowly.

1. Someone does the 'Argh'.

2. The person standing next to the raised arm says: 'Go!' and points left or right.

3. The person who is pointed at then points their fist at someone in the circle and says: 'Go!' and the name of the person they are pointing at.

4. That person then says: 'Argh!'

5. The person standing next to the raised hand says: 'Ni'.

6. Etcetera.

When the participants get familiar with the rules, add the following:

'When someone makes a mistake or takes longer than 3 seconds, they are out. The players who are out try to distract those still playing.'

Start the game. Be strict in applying the rules: everyone who makes a minor mistake is out. Applaud the winners.

Play the game a few times.

Comment

Play the game in a high tempo to increase the likelihood of mistakes.

PUSHING HANDS
You don't have to be strong to win

Energy level: medium
Number of participants: 2–50
Age: 8+

Time: 10 minutes
Materials: none

Explanation

Participants form pairs with someone who is about the same strength as themselves.

> 'Stand facing each other, feet together, approximately one arm's length apart.
>
> You are only allowed to touch each other's hands, but the objective is to unbalance your partner.
>
> The first one to lose their balance loses. When you are finished, find another partner.'

Debriefing

- What did you think about the exercise before you began?
- What did it feel like when you got out of balance because of your own force?

- How was it to win?

    - What value, if any, can you see in this game for dealing in power issues?

VARIATION

Bring variation by modifying the rules.

- Allow people to stand with legs apart.

- Hands have to be constantly in contact.

- You have 3 lives. When contests are over match people who have won 2 or 3 games against each other.

PARTICLE ACCELERATOR
Hear the signals moving around

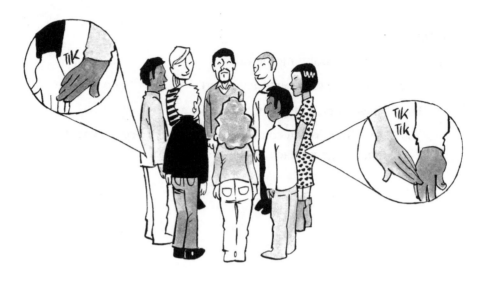

Energy level: medium

Number of participants: 8–50

Age: 8+

Time: 10 minutes

Materials: none

Explanation

Participants stand in a tight, closed circle.

> **'We are going to pass around a signal. I will tap the person to my left or right, then this person taps the person next to them. The goal is to pass the signal around the circle as quickly as possible. We play this game with our eyes closed.'**

Tap one of your neighbours and let the signal go around the circle a few times.

Make it more difficult by:

- giving one signal to the left and one to the right
- passing different signals such as a single tap and a double tap.

Comment

This activity can bring a pleasant kind of silence to the group. Usually participants mention that they enjoy listening to the sound.

COPY COPY

Imitate others whilst being imitated

Energy level: medium
Number of participants: 8–40
Age: 8+

Time: 10 minutes
Materials: none

Explanation

Participants stand in a circle.

> **'I want you to think of a pose you are going to adopt and then to pick someone in the group whose pose you are going to copy once you have done yours.'**

Demonstrate some poses as examples.

> **'On "3" I want you to adopt your pose, hold it for 3 breaths and then, in slow motion, change your pose to copy the person you chose.'**

Count to 3. Everyone assumes their pose, and after a few breaths everyone copies someone else.

This results in all participants moving in slow motion. Gradually people will become still. Their final positions will often be a blend of their initial pose and those that they have copied.

Comment

It is a good idea to demonstrate how to copy someone else's pose before you give the instruction. This way the participants will have a clearer idea of what is meant by copying in slow motion.

Debriefing

- How many different end positions do we have?
- How did it feel to do this exercise?
- How was it for you to follow someone else?
- Did you notice who was following you?
- Are there any similarities between this activity and consensus building in a group? If so, what are they?

COMMUNICATION

Communication is the process of exploring the relatedness between ourselves, others and the environment. It involves words, images, gesture, expression, tone, movement and more, in subtle and complex combinations.

In this chapter you will find a range of exercises that allow participants to consider different aspects of communication, using games as a medium.

Awareness is of crucial importance in learning and developing the skills involved in the following games. So it is necessary to allow time for debriefing to facilitate increased understanding, consideration and learning of the skills involved.

THE ORCHESTRA
Use body language to guide a group

Energy level: medium
Number of participants: 12–50
Age: 6+

Time: 30 minutes
Materials: instruments, chopstick

Explanation

Have a range of instruments, one for each participant. They can be improvised instruments from the kitchen, conventional ones or a mix of both.

Ask for a volunteer to be the conductor.

Each participant has an instrument and the conductor uses the chopstick to communicate with the orchestra.

'The musicians playing their instruments follow the instructions of the conductor, who indicates when the players start and stop.'

Let the music start.

The participants and conductor will gradually adapt to communicating in this way.

Stop the music after a few minutes and debrief.

Ask the conductor:

• What was it like to conduct?

- What went well?
- What would you like to do differently?

Ask the players:

- What was it like to play?
- What signals were clear?
- What could the conductor do differently?

If there is time, give the conductor a second opportunity to conduct.

The debriefing often generates a different quality of music, enhancing the communication between conductor and orchestra.

Allow different participants to be the conductor and support them in the following way:

- Before the orchestra plays, ask the conductor if they want to say something about what they expect from the performance.

- Have a quick debrief after a minute, checking what they feel or think is going well and what could be improved.

Comment

This exercise can be very exciting for the conductors. Leading a group of people can generate a range of feelings. In the debriefing it is valuable to focus on how the conductor experienced being in this role.

You can use this activity as a metaphor for harmony, difference and communication, perhaps asking how harmony in this exercise relates to harmony in everyday communication. Just as each instrument has its distinctive sound, we each have our own distinctive way of communicating, and also range of expression.

With young participants you take the role of the conductor first. This way you can tune the orchestra a bit. You can practise:

- when to start playing and when to stop
- playing louder and softer
- playing in a specific rhythm (march, waltz, slow, fast…) or without a rhythm.

Debriefing

You may begin by including the questions from the short debriefing above, but the following allow deeper reflection.

- What did you learn about communication through this exercise?
- Is there anything that you wanted to happen that you didn't manage to communicate?
- How did you experience that?
- What similarities do you see with this kind of communication and communication in daily life?
- What are the differences?

VARIATION 1

Instead of using an instrument the players use their voices or make sounds with their body (clapping, clicking fingers, rubbing hands…).

VARIATION 2

With a skilled group the conductor can experiment with conducting without using their hands to communicate with the orchestra.

CACOPHONY
Expressing feelings with your voice

Energy level: medium–high
Number of participants: 10–40
Age: 8+

Time: 10 minutes
Materials: none

Explanation

Participants stand or sit in a circle.

> 'I want you to think of a noise, sound or word that you can make for a few seconds, such as "wooowooo" or "labaralabara" or "meow" or "hoohuhuhoo". Decide on something yourself.'

First round: When all participants have chosen their sound, give the following instructions:

> 'Hold hands in a circle and someone begins by making their sound. When this person is ready they squeeze the hand of one of the people next to them. That person then makes their sound, then squeezes the next person's hand and continues to make their sound. In this way the sound builds as it carries on around the circle.'

Second round: Give the following instructions:

> **'Now make your sound and after 2 seconds you squeeze both your neighbours' hands. Both neighbours make their sound while you also continue with your sound.**
>
> **So every 2 seconds 2 more voices are added. When everyone is involved the person who began gives a double squeeze left and right. When you feel the double squeeze you stop making your sound after 2 more seconds, and then give a double squeeze to your neighbour.'**

So every 2 seconds the noise gets lower until there is silence.

Third round: Give the following instructions:

> **'Now I want you to make your sound with a particular emotion, for example, meowing in a sad or bored way.'**

The participants make their sounds in turn with a specific emotion, and the rest of the group tries to guess what emotion was being communicated.

Comment

In this activity participants practise the non-verbal aspects of communication using their voice. This activity can be an introduction for a workshop about using your voice to express what you want.

Debriefing

- Did you enjoy this game? What did you like about it?
- Was there anything difficult about it? What?
- What did you learn about communication through this exercise?
- Were you able to guess the emotion that people were trying to communicate through their noises?

CATS AND DOGS IN CONVERSATION

Express and receive feelings nonverbally

Energy level: high
Number of participants: 10–40
Age: 10+

Time: 10 minutes
Materials: copy of the emotional words sheet for each participant

Explanation

Download the template (see p.225) from www.jkp.com/catalogue/book/9781849051927/resources, print and give everyone an emotional words sheet. Participants get into pairs and sit back to back. One is a cat and the other a dog.

> **'Using only dog noises, communicate different emotions from your word sheet. Your partner tries to guess the emotion you are trying to communicate.**
>
> **First the dog tries to convey 3 emotions. Then you swap roles and the cat expresses 3 emotions.'**

Comment

This game can enrich the participants' emotional vocabulary. It can be used to explore the difference and importance of listening and speaking and the role of both in communication. It can also be helpful in looking at the need for subtlety in conveying emotion.

Debriefing

- How did you find the game?
- How successful were you at communicating the different emotions?
- How successful were you at guessing the emotion being expressed?
- Which emotions did you find it easy to express?
- Which emotions were more difficult to express?

Emotional words sheet

frightened   embarrassed   excited   shy

affectionate   fascinated   exasperated

sad   alarmed   tender   bewildered

resigned   distressed   disgusted   surprised

nervous   flirtatious   bored   loving

relaxed   eager   joyful   guilty   determined

despairing   passive   lonely   jealous

ashamed   enthusiastic   aloof   edgy

serene   grieving   frazzled   appreciative

anxious   dejected   puzzled   weary

contemptuous   depressed   trusting

proud annoyed   calm   miserable   modest

curious   gloomy   sensitive   amused

broken-hearted   friendly   impatient

resigned   horrified   angry   sexy

cold   sulky

 downloadable

SECRET SPOT

Find your own and others' secret location without talking

Energy level: medium
Number of participants: 6–40
Age: 10+

Time: 10 minutes
Materials: a newspaper

Explanation

Form groups of 5.

> 'I want each of you to think of a specific place in the room, but keep it secret from the rest of your group.'

Give each group a sheet of a newspaper.

> 'Everyone in the group hold the sheet with both hands, and keep your hands in the same place throughout the game.
>
> Now, without talking or tearing the newspaper, I want you to walk to your special place and stay there for at least 5 seconds. Each group has 5 minutes to visit all 5 secret locations. And remember, no talking, and don't tear the paper.'

When a group is finished they leave the newspaper on the ground and sit in the circle.

Comment

This is an ideal exercise to introduce the issue of dealing with conflict.

The game is a metaphor for conflicting needs among people. It shows that with openness, sensitivity and exploration among the different parties involved, it is possible to find creative solutions.

Debriefing

- Which groups managed to do the task?
- How did you communicate in your group?
- Do you know where your group members' special places are?
- How did you negotiate a sequence of going to the different places?
- What similarities do you see between this activity and dealing with apparently conflicting needs?
- What did you learn from this game for dealing with conflict?

YES/NO

Experience how your energy affects others

Energy level: medium–high
Number of participants: 6–40
Age: 10+

Time: 10 minutes
Materials: none

Explanation

The participants form pairs. In each pair, choose who will be A and who will be B.

> **'For 1 minute person A says "Yes", and person B responds "No".**
> **Start calm and see how the conversation evolves when you change**
> **your voice or your body language.'**

Usually you will hear the voices getting louder and louder. Stop the game after a minute.

Comment

Keep the conversation in a kind of ping-pong rhythm. This activity can be used as a warm-up for a deeper discussion or activity about themes such as differences between boys and girls, communication between parents and kids, teachers and students…

Debriefing

- How did you find this activity?
- In what way did you influence each other?
- What struck you in this game?
- Do you see similarities between this game and communication in real life? If so, what?

VARIATION 1

You can use other sentences like:

Person A	**Person B**
I don't want to.	You have to.
I go.	You stay.
Help me.	I can't.
The milk is cooking.	Take it off the stove.
The phone is ringing.	Pick it up.

VARIATION 2

One person plays the role of a teenager and the other person plays the role of the parent.

Suggest an issue to talk about: cleaning up, honesty, politeness, pocket money...

They each take it in turns to speak.

DEBRIEFING

- How did you find the role-play?
- Did it seem authentic?
- What are you learning from it?
- What is it that parents can learn from teenagers?
- What can teenagers learn from the parents?

VARIATION 3

Form 2 rows, each with a mix of boys and girls.

Each person partners up with the person opposite in the other row. The people on one side play the role of a boy and on the other a girl, regardless of their sex.

Suggest an issue to talk about:

- What makes a film good?
- What sports do you like and why?
- How does it feel to fall in love? (To discuss with older kids.)
- What things do you talk about with a friend?

They each take turns to speak.

DEBRIEFING

- Are there typical reactions for boys? If so, what?
- Are there typical reactions for girls? If so, what?
- Are there differences between the conversations of boys and girls?

FAST FIST FAST

Find a strategy to get what you want

Energy level: medium
Number of participants: 6–40
Age: 10+

Time: 10 minutes
Materials: none

Explanation

The participants form into pairs.

> **'One of you makes a fist. The objective is to open your partner's fist but you are not allowed to use any violence or to hurt the person in any way. So you will need to be creative.'**

Stop the game after a minute.

Usually half of the participants are successful.

Debriefing

- Who was successful in opening their partner's fist?

- Who wasn't successful?

- What helped to open their fist?

- What was the effect if someone used physical force?

- What did you learn from this exercise about getting what you want from someone?

THE WORLD'S WORST LISTENER

What does it feel like when someone doesn't listen?

Energy level: medium–high
Number of participants: 6–40
Age: 10+

Time: 10 minutes
Materials: stopwatch

Explanation

The participants form into pairs.

> **'Each pair decides on a subject that is easy to talk about.'**

When they all have a subject, give the following instruction.

> **'Now the tallest person in each pair speaks first about their subject for 1 minute and the other person acts like the world's worst listener, whilst remaining with their partner.'**

Give a signal to start.

After 1 minute partners change roles.

After the second round encourage the participants to try to break off from their partner in a friendly manner.

Debriefing

- What did you feel when the other person wasn't listening?
- What happened with your story?
- What did it feel like to be the bad listener?
- What signals made you think that the other person is not listening? (Record people's thoughts on a flipchart.)
- Where do you experience these 'bad-listener' signals in real life?
- When are you (an example of) a bad listener?
- What things help you pay attention more fully? (Record the ideas on a flipchart.)

VARIATION

Download and prepare cards for the 'bad listener' (from www.jkp.com/ catalogue/book/9781849051927/resources).

Two people do the exercise. Partner A tells a story and B is given a card that describes how they will engage with the story. The other participants observe.

After a minute the observers guess what instruction was given to the listener.

Have another pair perform the task, but with a different instruction card. Use the cards in numerical order. Once again the observers guess what they think the instruction is.

COMMENT

Use the debriefing to draw out the learning on listening:

- What do you think was on the card?
- How did you feel when the other listened like this?
- What have you learnt about good listening through doing or observing this exercise?
- How was it to listen according to the instructions?

For the last pair it is possible that the participants will think that there was a negative assignment on the instruction card. This feedback can be potentially embarrassing for the last listener (number 8), so choose the last pair with some thought as to their emotional robustness.

You may also experiment with other listening instructions relevant to your particular group and their needs.

The world's worst listener (Variation)

1. Pretend that you are listening. Meanwhile work out the following maths problem: 1 x 2 x 3 x 4 x 5 x 6 x 7 x 8 If you think you have the answer, say: 'Stop!'	**2.** Try to listen as well as possible but move your nose from the left to right as if you are saying 'No'.
3. Listen to what the other is saying but avoid any eye contact.	**4.** Listen to what the other is saying and repeat often what is said. Say at least 5 times: 'If I understand what you are saying, then…'
5. Try to steer what the other is saying by asking questions that move the story away from their intended direction.	**6.** Don't listen particularly to the words, but focus on and copy the body language and gestures.
7. Listen to the story but make verbal response words, or 'umm's and 'ah's louder than the speaker's.	**8.** Listen as well as you possibly can. Do whatever you think is appropriate to be a good listener.

SWAP SHOP
Follow a prescribed ritual in exchanging objects

Energy level: medium
Number of participants: 12–40
Age: 10+

Time: 10 minutes
Materials: none

Explanation

The participants stand in a circle.

> **'For this activity you will need a personal object to swap, such as a ring, a pen, a watch… Don't worry, you will get it back at the end.'**

When everyone has chosen an object, give the following instructions:

> **'Now I want you to swap your object with someone, observing the following ritual: approach a person, shake hands and say "Hi [name of the person], this is [your name]'s object." The other person does the same, following the ritual.**
>
> **When you have swapped objects, you then approach another person and once again shake hands and say "Hi [name of the person], this is [name]'s object." Except this time use the name of the person whose object it is.'**

Once everyone has heard and understood the instruction, they swap objects with 12–15 people.

After several minutes end the game and ask everyone to return the object to its rightful owner.

Comment

This is a good activity for introducing a discussion on listening skills.

It is important to give a clear demonstration of the form of the ritual at the start.

Debriefing

- Who was able to return the object to its owner straight away?
- Who had to ask before they could return the object?
- How did you find this activity?
- What skills did you need to do this activity?
- What strategies did you use to do the activity well?
- How does this activity relate to listening?

BISCUITS

Exploring issues of peer pressure

Energy level: medium
Number of participants: 8–40
Age: 10+
Time: 15 minutes

Materials: game cards (copy template), 1 pack of biscuits per 8 participants

Explanation

The participants form groups of 8, each group taking seats around a different table.

Download a copy of the template (see p.240) from www.jkp.com/catalogue/book/9781849051927/resources, print, cut the roles out, give each participant a 'role card' and put a pack of biscuits in the middle of each table.

> **'I want you to play the role that is on your card as well as possible until the end of the game.'**

Announce the start of the game.

The participant in each group with 'Role 1' will open the pack of biscuits and offer them around, but some participants will eat and some won't. Observe the interaction.

Stop the game after 5 minutes and form groups with people who had the same role, i.e. all those who had Role 1 together, and so on.

Comment

Choose biscuits that don't contain nuts or animal fats, and check if anyone is allergic to biscuits at the start.

Instead of biscuits you can use crisps. This will often trigger participants, especially when you do it before lunch or dinner.

Debriefing

The debriefing takes place in 2 stages: *first*, the participants reflect with others from the different groups who played the same role; *second*, debrief with the whole group.

Debriefing of the specific roles: Discuss the game using the following questions as a guideline, writing on an A1 sheet:

- What did it feel like to play your role?
- What role did the others play?
- What strategies helped you to play the role?
- What was difficult?

Debrief with the whole group in a circle:

- Who had an easy role? Why was it easy?
- Who had a difficult role? What made it difficult?
- How was it for the number 2s to say 'No'?
- Do you experience similar situations in real life? If so, what?

• What have you learnt through doing this activity?

> This game is designed to introduce the issues of peer pressure in the context of experimenting with drugs. It is important to focus the reflection not on drugs but rather on the positive skills you want to encourage. Do this with questions such as:
>
> • In which ways can you say no?
>
> • What worked for you?
>
> • What can you do if others keep on insisting that you try something you don't want to do?
>
> • How can you support others if you see that they are having trouble saying 'No'?

Biscuits

Role 1
Play this role as well as possible:
Open the pack of biscuits and offer everybody one.

Role 2
Play this role as well as possible:
Don't touch the biscuits even when they insist.

Role 3
Play this role as well as possible:
Encourage everyone to try at least one whole biscuit.

Role 4
Play this role as well as possible:
Eat only half a biscuit and leave the rest on the table.

Role 5
Play this role as well as possible:
Eat as many biscuits as you like.

Role 6
Play this role as well as possible:
Don't eat any biscuit yourself but encourage others to eat them.

Role 7
Play this role as well as possible:
Eat a biscuit now and then but discourage others from touching them.

Role 8
Play this role as well as possible:
Only eat a biscuit when everyone else has eaten at least one.

 downloadable

CHAIR GAME
Exploring issues of peer pressure

Energy level: (extreme) high
Number of participants: 8–40
Age: 10+

Time: 15 minutes
Materials: chair and chair game card
for each participant (template 1)

Explanation

Participants sit in chairs in a circle. Download copies of template 1 (see p.244) from www.jkp.com/catalogue/book/9781849051927/resources, print, cut out and give everyone a card.

> **'Read what is on your card, memorize it and put it away.**
>
> **The objective is to fulfil the task that is outlined on your card. The rules for this activity are:**
>
> - **respect for others, so don't hurt anyone**
>
> - **respect for materials, so don't break anything**
>
> - **don't show your card to anyone.'**

Announce the start of the game.

Usually participants start moving chairs in different directions. Sometimes participants start to communicate and work out a solution that meets everyone's needs.

If the chaos gets too intensive, stop the game and display a sheet with the following text: 'Try to find a solution that meet everyone's needs.' This impulse usually gives the participants the inspiration to talk about their task. Whatever the outcome is, debrief the activity.

Comment

This game is a great metaphor for conflict. It gives the participants the experience of how it feels to be in a conflict. The way participants deal with the game is always different.

In the debriefing, draw on specific events during the exercise to enhance the experiential learning possibilities for the group.

Using the game as a metaphor for conflicts in general, the participants can work out their own list of guidelines for dealing with conflict.

Debriefing

- What did it feel like doing this activity?
- Did you notice any changes during the game? If so, what?
- How many different tasks do you think there are?
- What made the conflict difficult?
- What helped you find a solution?
- Did you learn anything about solving conflicts? If so, what?

QUIET VARIATION

If you are concerned that the game will be too noisy, you can play the following variation. (Download, print and prepare a set of cards from template 2 on p.245.)

Put some tables together and have 9 participants sit around the table (with the others observing). In the middle of the table is a deck of playing cards. Each player has a task card that they must not show to anyone. There are 3 copies of each of the following 3 task cards:

- Put a quarter of the cards in each corner of the table. You have 7 minutes to complete this task.

- Make a large circle with the cards. You have 7 minutes to complete this task.

- Make a big arrow with the cards. You have 7 minutes to complete this task.

Give the following instructions:

'Keep one arm behind your back throughout the game and find a way to fulfil the instruction on your task card. You can negotiate with the others as necessary, but you must not show your task card to anyone.'

Usually the participants start impulsively, putting the cards where they want to have them. You may choose to offer either a verbal or a visual clue at some stage about the need to negotiate.

The debriefing usually gives the participants some insight into the nature of conflict and how it affects those involved.

Chair game 1

Put all the chairs in a circle.
You have 7 minutes to complete this task.

Put all the chairs in a circle.
You have 7 minutes to complete this task.

Put all the chairs in a circle.
You have 7 minutes to complete this task.

Put all the chairs by the window.
You have 7 minutes to complete this task.

Put all the chairs by the window.
You have 7 minutes to complete this task.

Put all the chairs by the window.
You have 7 minutes to complete this task.

Put all the chairs by the door.
You have 7 minutes to complete this task.

Put all the chairs by the door.
You have 7 minutes to complete this task.

Put all the chairs by the door.
You have 7 minutes to complete this task.

 downloadable

Chair game 2 (Quiet variation)

Put a quarter of the cards in each corner of the table.
You have 7 minutes to complete this task.

Put a quarter of the cards in each corner of the table.
You have 7 minutes to complete this task.

Put a quarter of the cards in each corner of the table.
You have 7 minutes to complete this task.

Make a large circle with the cards.
You have 7 minutes to complete this task.

Make a large circle with the cards.
 You have 7 minutes to complete this task.

Make a large circle with the cards.
You have 7 minutes to complete this task.

Make a big arrow with the cards.
You have 7 minutes to complete this task.

Make a big arrow with the cards.
You have 7 minutes to complete this task.

Make a big arrow with the cards.
You have 7 minutes to complete this task.

 downloadable

YOU OR ME?

Conflicting needs or not?

Energy level: medium
Number of participants: 8–40
Age: 10+

Time: 10 minutes
Materials: masking tape

Explanation

Make a line across the middle of the room with masking tape.

The task is an open one. There is no right answer or victory, and much of the value in the exercise is the debriefing of how the participants related to the task.

The participants form pairs, with one person on either side of the line.

> **'Now I want you to try to get your partner to cross over the line. You are not allowed to touch each other or to talk. When one or both of you have crossed the line, sit down and observe.'**

Give a signal to start the game.

Usually participants start miming that the other has to come over. During the game some participants will step over the line, some will remain standing on their original side and some will perhaps step over the line at the same point.

Stop the game after 5 to 7 minutes.

Comment

This game is a good warm-up for exploring apparently conflicting needs and finding creative solutions.

If both participants step over the line at the same time they both achieve their goal.

Debriefing

- Who stepped over the line? What made you do that?
- What strategies did you use to get your partner to cross the line?
- Which partners remained on their original sides? Why was that?
- Were there other solutions?
- What would you have said if you were able to talk?

You can discuss what is needed to find creative kinds of solutions and see if this is relevant to conflicts in real life. Participants often discover that solving conflicts requires:

- clarity over what you want yourself
- listening to what the other person needs
- exploring possible solutions before choosing one
- creativity, if it is clear what both parties finally want to achieve, what the underlying needs are.

TEXT HATS

Experience what it feels like to have people reacting to you in an unfamiliar way

Energy level: medium
Number of participants: 6–30
Age: 12+
Time: 20 minutes

Materials: text hats (made from suitably strong paper, e.g. 100g/m² with some text written clearly on it)

Explanation

Prepare a text hat for each participant.

Use one text for each group you want – so, for example, if you want to make 4 groups, use 4 texts.

Ideas for texts:

- Smile at me.
- I stink.
- Show your tongue.
- I am dangerous.
- Don't look at me.
- Admire me.
- Look at me from head to toe.

- Look at me but not into my eyes.

  - Only look at me when I'm not looking at you.

Participants sit in a circle.

Put a hat on each participant. Then allow time for them just to look at each other before beginning the exercise.

'Now stand up and walk around the room, using all the space. React to each other according to the message on the other person's hat but don't talk, only use body language to communicate.'

Let the participants experience the effect of the hats for 2 minutes.

'Now form groups with participants you think are wearing the same hat as yourself.'

Allow time for the participants to discuss what it felt like to engage in this activity.

Comment

This game is a good introduction for a workshop about:

- self-esteem
- how I feel when people look at me
- how my self-esteem or lack of it affects my confidence to meet new people or situations
- the beliefs I have about myself and how to deal with others
- exploring difference and diversity.

Debriefing

- How was it to play this game?
- Who enjoyed their role? What did you enjoy?
- Who didn't enjoy their role? What was it you didn't like?

EVALUATING AND PARTING

Most of the activities in this book have specific debriefing questions and reflections. At the conclusion of a session or workshop, or at the end of a group, it is valuable to have an evaluation to facilitate the completion of both the learning and the parting processes.

In this chapter you will find activities and ideas to help with the process of completion.

EVALUATE WITH SYMBOLS
Quick evaluation forms

Energy level: low
Number of participants: 6–50
Age: 6+

Time: 5 minutes
Materials: large sheets of paper, pens, coloured pencils

Explanation

The participants sit or stand in a circle.

Name an aspect, or part, of the workshop and ask the participants to give their evaluation in a manner described, for example:

'Say in one word how you found the food.

Show with a movement of one or both hands how the morning activity was for you.

Show with a facial expression how you found the afternoon activity.

Using a sound, but not words, communicate how you found the evening activity.

Mime how you felt in the group.

Describe how you are feeling after the session, using a colour.'

Comment

To evaluate in this way you can ask someone to begin, moving clockwise around the circle, and those that wish to pass can pass. Or you can ask who would like to start, and then ask if it is okay to continue around in order. A third option is for people just to participate when they are ready.

This last method takes more time but encourages active participation from group members, and also allows those who might wish to pass to remain less conspicuous, thereby supporting their emotional safety.

It is important to value people's feedback and experience. Avoid asking someone specifically to explain their evaluation, but you could ask if anyone wants to comment on their feedback.

VARIATION 1

If you want the evaluation to be low-risk, you can ask participants to respond all at the same time. You will then have a general idea how that aspect was evaluated.

VARIATION 2

Form groups of 5 and list the different aspects you want them to evaluate. In each group the participants give points from 0 to 5, with 5 being the best, and someone in each group keeps a record of the scores. The groups discuss the scores they have and comment on their experience. In a plenary session a spokesperson from each group gives the scores and a summary of the group's discussion.

VARIATION 3

For the evaluation of an ongoing workshop, divide into groups of 5. Each group designs a graph of the evolution of their learning process. The bottom line indicates the time (weeks, months) and the vertical line indicates the level of learning, enjoyment, engagement…

Give some examples, such as the first sessions, significant events and subjects covered, which you would like the group to illustrate in their graphics. Each participant can add comments in different colours. In a plenary session a spokesperson from each group elucidates the graphs.

VARIATION 4: 'WEATHER FORECAST'

The participants sit in a circle.

> 'Look inside and see how you are feeling, then express that using a sentence from a weather forecast.'

Go around the whole group and, as always, it is okay to pass.

COMMENT

This last variation is a good way to start a day with participants who know each other already. Sharing feelings in the vocabulary of a weather forecast makes it more playful and less serious.

BACKING SUPPORT
Giving written compliments

Energy level: medium
Number of participants: 6–50
Age: 8+
Time: 15 minutes

Materials: masking tape; 1 cardboard sheet and 1 coloured marker pen per participant

Explanation

Each person has a cardboard sheet attached to their back with masking tape. The participants then stand in a circle, each with a coloured marker pen.

> **'I want you to write what you appreciate about someone on their sheet. You can thank them for something, or you can write a warm wish. Endeavour to write only what is true and comes from your heart, and try to write something on everyone's sheet.'**

Give the group about 10 minutes to write messages on each others' backs and encourage the group to make sure each participant receives a number of comments.

Ask the group to stand in a circle to finish the exercise.

Comment

This activity can only be done when there is a warm, respectful climate in the group. In groups of younger people it is important to ensure everyone takes the exercise seriously.

Debriefing

- How did it feel to give a compliment? To know how it feels *receiving* compliments and feedback, they now have to remove their sheet and read it.

- Participants take off their sheets and read them.

- How is it to read this sheet?

- What are you going to do with the sheet?

VARIATION 1

Participants sit in circles of about 6–10 people, each person with a pen and a sheet of paper.

'Write your name clearly at the bottom of your sheet of paper.'

Wait for the participants to write their names on the bottom of the sheet.

'Now pass your sheet to the person on your left. Spend 2 minutes just looking at the person whose name is on the sheet you are holding, then spend 2 minutes writing down your thoughts, appreciations and celebrations of this person. Write at the top of the sheet so there is space for more. Only write down positive comments and feedback.'

Call time after 4 minutes.

'Now fold the paper so that the next person can't see what is written, and pass it to the person on your left.'

Repeat the procedure, allowing 4 minutes for looking and writing. In this way, the papers go around the group and each participant shares some written appreciation on the sheet.

The papers will finally arrive at the person to the right of the person whose name is on the sheet. After adding their own comments the neighbour unfolds the sheet, reads everything that is written to the person and hands them the sheet. This is done in turn so that everyone can hear.

VARIATION 2

Hang sheets of paper on the walls (either A1, A2 or A3), with one sheet for each group member.

> **'Write your name at the top of one sheet and then move around the room and write, or draw, something on other group members' sheets.'**

After 10 minutes call time and then allow 5 minutes for people to look at others' sheets. Then ask people how they feel to see what people have written or drawn in relation to themselves or each other.

VARIATION 3

In groups of 3 to 5, people sit in a circle and think of an image for each member of their group. When everyone is ready, take it in turns to describe the image you have chosen and explain why. Divide the time equally among all the group members. Bring the whole group back for a final session.

FEEL-O-METER
A quick method for gauging the feelings and thoughts of a group

Energy level: low
Number of participants: 6–600
Age: 8+

Time: 2 minutes
Materials: none

Explanation

Demonstrate how you want participants to give their evaluation on aspects of the workshop: a hand held high in the air means 'very much', a hand held low means 'not at all' and a hand in the middle means 'more or less'.

Participants always give their evaluation with eyes closed so that they don't get influenced by others. Everyone can open their eyes after you have counted to 3.

> **'Close your eyes and give your evaluation on the following: How much did I enjoy the games at the start of the workshop?'**

Count to 3 slowly, and then the participants can open their eyes.

After every round you can consider asking if anyone would like to comment on their evaluation. Repeat the form with other sentences, such as:

> **'How much did the workshop meet my expectations?'**

> **'How much did I feel connected with others?'**

'How much did I enjoy the session?'

'How likely am I to do another workshop?'

Comment

This method can also be used at the start of a session to ascertain the group's experience for the subject you are going to explore. For example, **'Indicate the level of your knowledge or experience of this subject.'**

It is useful to get the group to close their eyes to engage with the question more from their own perspective. Also, you will find a wider range of expressions from low to high.

WITH AN IMAGE
Using a picture to reflect on my role in the group

Energy level: low
Number of participants: 6–40
Age: 8+
Time: 30 minutes

Materials: copy of one (age-appropriate set) of pictures for each participant (enlarge sheet size to A3 in the printer dialogue box)

Explanation

Download the pictures from www.jkp.com/catalogue/book/978184905 1927/resources, print and give every participant a copy of one of the pictures, using the first ones for younger participants. The last one is a picture inspired by Leary's Rose (Timothy Leary, American Psychologist) and is suitable for more mature participants.

> 'Look at the figures in the picture. If this was a picture of our group, where do you see yourself? Or if you don't see yourself, where would you picture yourself? Or maybe there is a figure that shows how you would like to have been in the group.
>
> Do you see other group members in the picture?
>
> Take some drawing materials and colour or draw figures that have things you recognize in yourself. You can also add some text balloons.
>
> Also mark out the figures that make you think of people in the group.'

When the participants are ready, form pairs (or 4s or 6s).

> **'Share with each other how you see yourself and others in the group, using the picture as a guide. You have 6 minutes, so take care to divide the time equally.'**

Change partners twice, to share with different people.

Debriefing

- How was it to find yourself in the picture?
- How was it to see others in the picture?
- How did you find exchanging ideas in pairs?
- What did you learn about our group and your role in it?

VARIATION

Give each participant a block of clay.

> **'Recall the workshop we had and use the clay to create a figure or form that shows how you found the workshop and what you got from it.'**

When the participants are ready with their sculptures, place them in the centre and sit around them.

View each sculpture in turn and allow the participants to say what they see in the object. Then give the creator an opportunity to say what they were trying to portray.

Suitable for age 8–11.

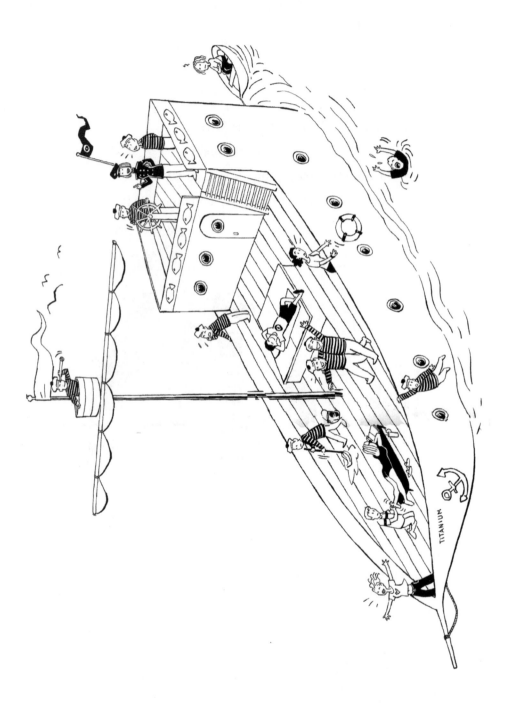

Suitable for age 10–14.

downloadable

Suitable for age 12–80.

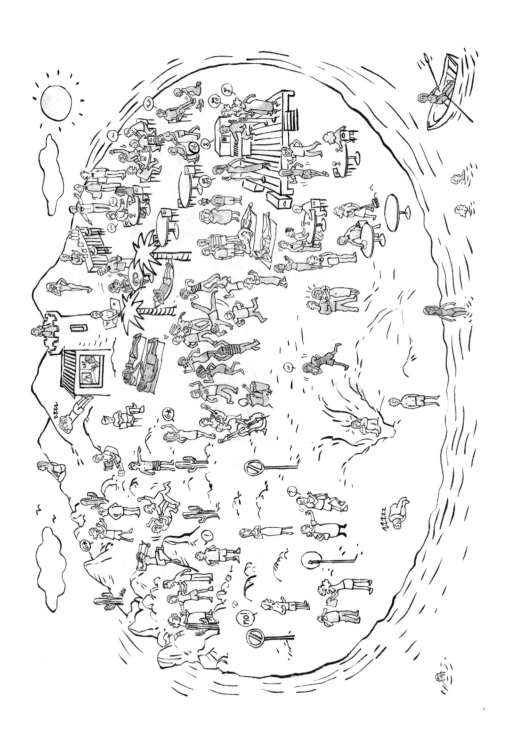

CREATIVE FAREWELL
Saying goodbye in a genuine way

Energy level: medium
Number of participants: 12–40
Age: 8+

Time: 10 minutes
Materials: none

Explanation

The participants stand in a circle.

> 'At the beginning of the workshop/school year we invested time to get to know each other. Before we leave I want to invite everyone to say goodbye to at least 7 people in the group in a genuine, authentic and creative way. I will give you some examples for inspiration.'

Demonstrate the following suggestions with a participant:

> 'You can shake hands and express your gratitude and what you have to say with words.
>
> You can greet each other as Buddhist monks and share your well-wishing and thoughts in a silent way.
>
> You can give the other one, 2 or 3 kisses on the cheek, checking beforehand to see if the other person is okay with this.
>
> You can rub noses like Eskimos.
>
> You can give a Russian hug.

You can do it in a creative way like teenagers.' (Give a demonstration of an elaborate handshake, fist bump, hand clap…)

'How you say goodbye is not as important as doing it in an authentic way with respect for the other person.'

Usually the participants start spontaneously hugging and greeting each other. There is no formal end to the activity.

Comment

As community-building games give the participants extra stimulation and inspiration, this game gives an extra impulse to enjoy saying goodbye and thanking and celebrating each other. This energizer is a good end for a workshop or session where people have been in positive, intimate contact with each other.

STAR EVALUATION
Showing your evaluation spatially

Energy level: medium
Number of participants: 12+
Age: 8+

Time: 10 minutes
Materials: personal props

Explanation

The participants sit in a circle. Put a stone (or other object) in the middle of the circle. Each participant needs a personal object. Explain that you want to evaluate some topics of the workshop/school year…

> **'When I say a sentence about an aspect of the workshop, you place your object nearer or further away from the object in the centre. The closer your object is to the centre, the more you agree with the statement; the further away, the more you disagree.'**

Possible evaluation statements (beginning with less challenging questions):

- The food was great.
- The pudding was the best ever.
- I slept well.
- I am happy to go home.
- I enjoyed the atmosphere in the group.

- I felt respected by everyone.
- I learned a lot I can use.
- The programme exceeded my expectations.
- Al my questions are answered.

After participants have placed their object, invite people to express why they placed it where they did.

VARIATION 1

Instead of placing an object, the participants can move closer to, or further away from, the centre of the circle to show their agreement or disagreement with the statement.

VARIATION 2

A participant can step into the centre of the circle and invite people to demonstrate their agreement or disagreement with a statement by moving closer to, or further away from, the centre.

ALPHABETICAL LIST OF THE ENERGIZER GAMES